The Revolt Of Islam by Percy Bysshe Shelley

A POEM IN TWELVE CANTOS.

Percy Bysshe Shelley is one of the most revered figures in the English poetical landscape. Born on the 4th August 1792 he has, over the years, become rightly regarded as a major Romantic poet. Yet during his own lifetime little of his work was published. Publishers feared his radical views and possible charges against themselves for blasphemy and sedition. On 8th July 1822 a month before his 30th birthday, during a sudden storm, his tragic early death by drowning robbed our culture of many fine expected masterpieces. But in his short spell on earth he weaved much magic. Among his many great works is The Revolt Of Islam. Shelley's words are alive with intent, meaning and emotion. A true poet for all our ages.

Index Of Contents
Author's Preface
Dedication
To Mary
CANTO 1.
CANTO 2
CANTO 3
CANTO 4
CANTO 5
CANTO 6
CANTO 7
CANTO 8
CANTO 9
CANTO 10
CANTO 11
CANTO 12
Note on the "REVOLT OF ISLAM", by Mrs Shelley
Percy Bysshe Shelley to Mary Godwin
A Note On The Poem's Composition

AUTHOR'S PREFACE.

The Poem which I now present to the world is an attempt from which I scarcely dare to expect success, and in which a writer of established fame might fail without disgrace. It is an experiment on the temper of the public mind, as to how far a thirst for a happier condition of moral and political society survives, among the enlightened and refined, the tempests which have shaken the age in which we live. I have sought to enlist the harmony of metrical language, the ethereal combinations of the fancy, the rapid and subtle transitions of human passion, all those elements which essentially compose a Poem, in the cause of a liberal and comprehensive morality; and in the view of kindling within the bosoms of my readers a virtuous enthusiasm for those doctrines of liberty and justice, that faith and hope in something good, which neither violence nor misrepresentation nor prejudice can ever totally extinguish among mankind.

For this purpose I have chosen a story of human passion in its most universal character, diversified with moving and romantic adventures, and appealing, in contempt of all artificial opinions or institutions, to the common sympathies of every human breast. I have made no attempt to recommend the motives which I would substitute for those at present governing mankind, by methodical and systematic argument. I would only awaken the feelings, so that the reader should see the beauty of true virtue, and be incited to those inquiries which have led to my moral and political creed, and that of some of the sublimest intellects in the world. The Poem therefore (with the exception of the first canto, which is purely introductory) is narrative, not didactic. It is a succession of pictures illustrating the growth and progress of individual mind aspiring after excellence, and devoted to the love of mankind; its influence in refining and making pure the most daring and uncommon impulses of the imagination, the understanding, and the senses; its impatience at 'all the oppressions which are done under the sun;' its tendency to awaken public hope, and to enlighten and improve mankind; the rapid effects of the application of that tendency; the awakening of an immense nation from their slavery and degradation to a true sense of moral dignity and freedom; the bloodless dethronement of their oppressors, and the unveiling of the religious frauds by which they had been deluded into submission; the tranquillity of successful patriotism, and the universal toleration and benevolence of true philanthropy; the treachery and barbarity of hired soldiers; vice not the object of punishment and hatred, but kindness and pity; the faithlessness of tyrants; the confederacy of the Rulers of the World and the restoration of the expelled Dynasty by foreign arms; the massacre and extermination of the Patriots, and the victory of established power; the consequences of legitimate despotism, civil war, famine, plague, superstition, and an utter extinction of the domestic affections; the judicial murder of the advocates of Liberty; the temporary triumph of oppression, that secure earnest of its final and inevitable fall; the transient nature of ignorance and error and the eternity of genius and virtue. Such is the series of delineations of which the Poem consists. And, if the lofty passions with which it has been my scope to distinguish this story shall not excite in the reader a generous impulse, an ardent thirst for excellence, an interest profound and strong such as belongs to no meaner desires, let not the failure be imputed to a natural unfitness for human sympathy in these sublime and animating themes. It is the business of the Poet to communicate to others the pleasure and the enthusiasm arising out of those images and feelings in the vivid presence of which within his own mind consists at once his inspiration and his reward.

The panic which, like an epidemic transport, seized upon all classes of men during the excesses consequent upon the French Revolution, is gradually giving place to sanity. It has ceased to be believed that whole generations of mankind ought to consign themselves to a hopeless inheritance of ignorance and misery, because a nation of men who had been dupes and slaves for centuries were incapable of conducting themselves with the wisdom and tranquillity of freemen so soon as some of their fetters were partially loosened. That their conduct could not have been marked by any other characters than ferocity and thoughtlessness is the historical fact from which liberty derives all its recommendations, and falsehood the worst features of its deformity. There is a reflux in the tide of human things which bears the shipwrecked hopes of men into a secure haven after the storms are past. Methinks, those who now live have survived an age of despair.

The French Revolution may be considered as one of those manifestations of a general state of feeling among civilised mankind produced by a defect of correspondence between the knowledge existing in society and the improvement or gradual abolition of political institutions. The year 1788 may be assumed as the epoch of one of the most important crises produced by this feeling. The sympathies connected with that event extended to every bosom. The most generous and amiable natures were those which participated the most extensively in these sympathies. But such a degree of unmingled good was expected as it was impossible to realise. If the Revolution had been in every respect prosperous, then misrule and superstition would lose half their claims to our abhorrence, as fetters which the captive can unlock with the slightest motion of his fingers, and which do not eat with poisonous rust into the soul. The revulsion occasioned by the atrocities of the demagogues, and the re-establishment of successive tyrannies in France, was terrible, and felt in the remotest corner of the civilised world. Could they listen to the plea of reason who had groaned under the calamities of a social state according to the provisions of which one man riots in luxury whilst another famishes for want of bread? Can he who the day before was a trampled slave suddenly become liberal-minded, forbearing, and independent? This is the consequence of the habits of a state of society to be produced by resolute perseverance and indefatigable hope, and long-suffering and long-believing courage, and the systematic efforts of generations of men of intellect and virtue. Such is the lesson which experience teaches now. But, on the first reverses of hope in the progress of French liberty, the sanguine eagerness for good overleaped the solution of these questions, and for a time extinguished itself in the unexpectedness of their result. Thus, many of the most ardent and tender-hearted of the worshippers of public good have been morally ruined by what a partial glimpse of the events they deplored appeared to show as the melancholy desolation of all their cherished hopes. Hence gloom and misanthropy have become the characteristics of the age in which we live, the solace of a disappointment that unconsciously finds relief only in the wilful exaggeration of its own despair. This influence has tainted the literature of the age with the hopelessness of the minds from which it flows. Metaphysics (I ought to except sir W. Drummond's "Academical Questions"; a volume of very acute and powerful metaphysical criticism.), and inquiries into moral and political science, have become little else than vain attempts to revive exploded superstitions, or sophisms like those of Mr. Malthus (It is remarkable, as a symptom of the revival of public hope, that Mr. Malthus has assigned, in the later editions of his work, an indefinite dominion to moral restraint over the principle of population. This concession answers all the inferences from his doctrine unfavourable to human improvement, and reduces the "Essay on Population" to a commentary illustrative of the unanswerableness of "Political Justice".), calculated to lull the oppressors of mankind into a security of everlasting triumph. Our works of fiction and poetry have been overshadowed by the same infectious gloom. But mankind appear to me to be emerging from their trance. I am aware, methinks, of a slow, gradual, silent change. In that belief I have composed the following Poem.

I do not presume to enter into competition with our greatest contemporary Poets. Yet I am unwilling to tread in the footsteps of any who have preceded me. I have sought to avoid the imitation of any style of language or versification peculiar to the original minds of which it is the character; designing that, even if what I have produced be worthless, it should still be properly my own. Nor have I permitted any system relating to mere words to divert the attention of the reader, from whatever interest I may have succeeded in creating, to my own ingenuity in contriving to disgust them according to the rules of criticism. I have simply clothed my thoughts in what appeared to me the most obvious and appropriate language. A person familiar with nature, and with the most celebrated productions of the human mind, can scarcely err in following the instinct, with respect to selection of language, produced by that familiarity.

There is an education peculiarly fitted for a Poet, without which genius and sensibility can hardly fill the circle of their capacities. No education, indeed, can entitle to this appellation a dull and unobservant mind, or one, though neither dull nor unobservant, in which the channels of communication between thought and expression have been obstructed or closed. How far it is my fortune to belong to either of the latter classes I cannot know. I aspire to be something better. The circumstances of my accidental education have been favourable to this ambition. I have been familiar from boyhood with mountains and lakes and the sea, and the solitude of forests: Danger, which sports upon the brink of precipices, has been my playmate. I have trodden the glaciers of the Alps, and lived under the eye of Mont Blanc. I have been a wanderer among distant fields. I have sailed down mighty rivers, and seen the sun rise and set, and the stars come forth, whilst I have sailed night and day down a rapid stream among mountains. I have seen populous cities, and have watched the passions which rise and spread, and sink and change, amongst assembled multitudes of men. I have seen the theatre of the more visible ravages of tyranny and war, cities and villages reduced to scattered groups of black and roofless houses, and the naked inhabitants sitting famished upon their desolated thresholds. I have conversed with living men of genius. The poetry of ancient Greece and Rome, and modern Italy, and our own country, has been to me, like external nature, a passion and an enjoyment. Such are the sources from which the materials for the imagery of my Poem have been drawn. I have considered Poetry in its most comprehensive sense; and have read the Poets and the Historians and the Metaphysicians (In this sense there may be such a thing as perfectibility in works of fiction, notwithstanding the concession often made by the advocates of human improvement, that perfectibility is a term applicable only to science.) whose writings have been accessible to me, and have looked upon the beautiful and majestic scenery of the earth, as common sources of those elements which it is the province of the Poet to embody and combine. Yet the experience and the feelings to which I refer do not in themselves constitute men Poets, but only prepares them to be the auditors of those who are. How far I shall be found to possess that more essential attribute of Poetry, the power of awakening in others sensations like those which animate my own bosom, is that which, to speak sincerely, I know not; and which, with an acquiescent and contented spirit, I expect to be taught by the effect which I shall produce upon those whom I now address.

I have avoided, as I have said before, the imitation of any contemporary style. But there must be a resemblance, which does not depend upon their own will, between all the writers of any particular age. They cannot escape from subjection to a common influence which arises out of an infinite combination of circumstances belonging to the times in which they live; though each is in a degree the author of the very influence by which his being is thus pervaded. Thus, the tragic poets of the age of Pericles; the Italian revivers of ancient learning; those mighty intellects of our own country that succeeded the Reformation, the translators of the Bible, Shakespeare, Spenser, the Dramatists of the reign of Elizabeth, and Lord Bacon (Milton stands alone in the age which he illumined.); the colder spirits of the interval that succeeded; all resemble each other, and differ from every other in their several classes. In this view of things, Ford can no more be called the imitator of Shakespeare than Shakespeare the imitator of Ford. There were perhaps few other points of resemblance between these two men than that which the universal and inevitable influence of their age produced. And this is an influence which neither the meanest scribbler nor the sublimest genius of any era can escape; and which I have not attempted to escape.

I have adopted the stanza of Spenser (a measure inexpressibly beautiful), not because I consider it a finer model of poetical harmony than the blank verse of Shakespeare and Milton, but because in the latter there is no shelter for mediocrity; you must either succeed or fail. This perhaps an aspiring spirit should desire. But I was enticed also by the brilliancy and magnificence of sound which a mind that has been nourished upon musical thoughts can produce by a just and harmonious arrangement of the pauses of this measure. Yet there will be found some instances where I have completely failed in this attempt, and one, which I here request the reader to consider as an erratum, where there is left, most inadvertently, an alexandrine in the middle of a stanza.

But in this, as in every other respect, I have written fearlessly. It is the misfortune of this age that its Writers, too thoughtless of immortality, are exquisitely sensible to temporary praise or blame. They write with the fear of Reviews before their eyes. This system of criticism sprang up in that torpid interval when Poetry was not. Poetry, and the art which professes to regulate and limit its powers, cannot subsist together. Longinus could not have been the contemporary of Homer, nor Boileau of Horace. Yet this species of criticism never presumed to assert an understanding of its own; it has always, unlike true science, followed, not preceded, the opinion of mankind, and would even now bribe with worthless adulation some of our greatest Poets to impose gratuitous fetters on their own imaginations, and become unconscious accomplices in the daily murder of all genius either not so aspiring or not so fortunate as their own. I have sought therefore to write, as I believe that Homer, Shakespeare, and Milton wrote, with an utter disregard of anonymous censure. I am certain that calumny and misrepresentation, though it may move me to compassion, cannot disturb my peace. I shall understand the expressive silence of those sagacious enemies who dare not trust themselves to speak. I shall endeavour to extract, from the midst of insult and contempt and maledictions, those admonitions which may tend to correct whatever imperfections such censurers may discover in this my first serious appeal to the Public. If certain Critics were as clear-sighted as they are malignant, how great would be the benefit to be derived from their virulent writings! As it is, I fear I shall be malicious enough to be amused with their paltry tricks and lame invectives. Should the Public judge that my composition is worthless, I shall indeed bow before the tribunal from which Milton received his crown of immortality, and shall seek to gather, if I live, strength from that defeat, which may nerve me to some new enterprise of thought which may not be worthless. I cannot conceive that Lucretius, when he meditated that poem whose doctrines are yet the basis of our metaphysical knowledge, and whose eloquence has been the wonder of mankind, wrote in awe of such censure as the hired sophists of the impure and superstitious noblemen of Rome might affix to what he should produce. It was at the period when Greece was led captive and Asia made tributary to the Republic, fast verging itself to slavery and ruin, that a multitude of Syrian captives, bigoted to the worship of their obscene Ashtaroth, and the unworthy successors of Socrates and Zeno, found there a precarious subsistence by administering, under the name of freedmen, to the vices and vanities of the great. These wretched men were skilled to plead, with a superficial but plausible set of sophisms, in favour of that contempt for virtue which is the portion of slaves, and that faith in portents, the most fatal substitute for benevolence in the imaginations of men, which, arising from the enslaved communities of the East, then first began to overwhelm the western nations in its stream. Were these the kind of men whose disapprobation the wise and lofty-minded Lucretius should have regarded with a salutary awe? The latest and perhaps the meanest of those who follow in his footsteps would disdain to hold life on such conditions.

The Poem now presented to the Public occupied little more than six months in the composition. That period has been devoted to the task with unremitting ardour and enthusiasm. I have exercised a watchful and earnest criticism on my work as it grew under my hands. I would willingly have sent it forth to the world with that perfection which long labour and revision is said to bestow. But I found that, if I should gain something in exactness by this method, I might lose much of the newness and energy of imagery and language as it flowed fresh from my mind. And, although the mere composition occupied no more than six months, the thoughts thus arranged were slowly gathered in as many years.

I trust that the reader will carefully distinguish between those opinions which have a dramatic propriety in reference to the characters which they are designed to elucidate, and such as are properly my own. The erroneous and degrading idea which men have conceived of a Supreme Being, for instance, is spoken against, but not the Supreme Being itself. The belief which some superstitious persons whom I have brought upon the stage entertain of the Deity, as injurious to the character of his benevolence, is widely different from my own. In recommending also a great and important change in the spirit which animates the social institutions of mankind, I have avoided all flattery to those violent and malignant passions of our nature which are ever on the watch to mingle with and to alloy the most beneficial innovations. There is no quarter given to Revenge, or Envy, or Prejudice. Love is celebrated everywhere as the sole law which should govern the moral world.

DEDICATION.
There is no danger to a man that knows
What life and death is: there's not any law
Exceeds his knowledge; neither is it lawful
That he should stoop to any other law. CHAPMAN.

TO MARY.

1.
So now my summer-task is ended, Mary,
And I return to thee, mine own heart's home;
As to his Queen some victor Knight of Faery,

Earning bright spoils for her enchanted dome;
Nor thou disdain, that ere my fame become
A star among the stars of mortal night,
If it indeed may cleave its natal gloom,
Its doubtful promise thus I would unite
With thy beloved name, thou Child of love and light.

2.
The toil which stole from thee so many an hour,
Is ended, and the fruit is at thy feet!
No longer where the woods to frame a bower
With interlaced branches mix and meet,
Or where with sound like many voices sweet,
Waterfalls leap among wild islands green,
Which framed for my lone boat a lone retreat
Of moss-grown trees and weeds, shall I be seen;
But beside thee, where still my heart has ever been.

3.
Thoughts of great deeds were mine, dear Friend, when first
The clouds which wrap this world from youth did pass.
I do remember well the hour which burst
My spirit's sleep. A fresh May-dawn it was,
When I walked forth upon the glittering grass,
And wept, I knew not why; until there rose
From the near schoolroom, voices that, alas!
Were but one echo from a world of woes
The harsh and grating strife of tyrants and of foes.

4.
And then I clasped my hands and looked around
But none was near to mock my streaming eyes,
Which poured their warm drops on the sunny ground
So without shame I spake: 'I will be wise,
And just, and free, and mild, if in me lies
Such power, for I grow weary to behold
The selfish and the strong still tyrannise
Without reproach or check.' I then controlled
My tears, my heart grew calm, and I was meek and bold.

5.
And from that hour did I with earnest thought
Heap knowledge from forbidden mines of lore;
Yet nothing that my tyrants knew or taught
I cared to learn, but from that secret store
Wrought linked armour for my soul, before
It might walk forth to war among mankind;

Thus power and hope were strengthened more and more
Within me, till there came upon my mind
A sense of loneliness, a thirst with which I pined.

6.
Alas, that love should be a blight and snare
To those who seek all sympathies in one!
Such once I sought in vain; then black despair,
The shadow of a starless night, was thrown
Over the world in which I moved alone:
Yet never found I one not false to me,
Hard hearts, and cold, like weights of icy stone
Which crushed and withered mine, that could not be
Aught but a lifeless clod, until revived by thee.

7.
Thou Friend, whose presence on my wintry heart
Fell, like bright Spring upon some herbless plain;
How beautiful and calm and free thou wert
In thy young wisdom, when the mortal chain
Of Custom thou didst burst and rend in twain,
And walked as free as light the clouds among,
Which many an envious slave then breathed in vain
From his dim dungeon, and my spirit sprung
To meet thee from the woes which had begirt it long!

8.
No more alone through the world's wilderness,
Although I trod the paths of high intent,
I journeyed now: no more companionless,
Where solitude is like despair, I went.
There is the wisdom of a stern content
When Poverty can blight the just and good,
When Infamy dares mock the innocent,
And cherished friends turn with the multitude
To trample: this was ours, and we unshaken stood!

9.
Now has descended a serener hour,
And with inconstant fortune, friends return;
Though suffering leaves the knowledge and the power
Which says: Let scorn be not repaid with scorn.
And from thy side two gentle babes are born
To fill our home with smiles, and thus are we
Most fortunate beneath life's beaming morn;
And these delights, and thou, have been to me
The parents of the Song I consecrate to thee.

10.
Is it that now my inexperienced fingers
But strike the prelude of a loftier strain?
Or, must the lyre on which my spirit lingers
Soon pause in silence, ne'er to sound again,
Though it might shake the Anarch Custom's reign,
And charm the minds of men to Truth's own sway
Holier than was Amphion's? I would fain
Reply in hope but I am worn away,
And Death and Love are yet contending for their prey.

11.
And what art thou? I know, but dare not speak:
Time may interpret to his silent years.
Yet in the paleness of thy thoughtful cheek,
And in the light thine ample forehead wears,
And in thy sweetest smiles, and in thy tears,
And in thy gentle speech, a prophecy
Is whispered, to subdue my fondest fears:
And through thine eyes, even in thy soul I see
A lamp of vestal fire burning internally.

12.
They say that thou wert lovely from thy birth,
Of glorious parents thou aspiring Child.
I wonder not, for One then left this earth
Whose life was like a setting planet mild,
Which clothed thee in the radiance undefiled
Of its departing glory; still her fame
Shines on thee, through the tempests dark and wild
Which shake these latter days; and thou canst claim
The shelter, from thy Sire, of an immortal name.

13.
One voice came forth from many a mighty spirit,
Which was the echo of three thousand years;
And the tumultuous world stood mute to hear it,
As some lone man who in a desert hears
The music of his home: unwonted fears
Fell on the pale oppressors of our race,
And Faith, and Custom, and low-thoughted cares,
Like thunder-stricken dragons, for a space
Left the torn human heart, their food and dwelling-place.

14.
Truth's deathless voice pauses among mankind!

If there must be no response to my cry
If men must rise and stamp with fury blind
On his pure name who loves them, thou and I,
Sweet friend! can look from our tranquillity
Like lamps into the world's tempestuous night,
Two tranquil stars, while clouds are passing by
Which wrap them from the foundering seaman's sight,
That burn from year to year with unextinguished light.

CANTO 1.

1.
When the last hope of trampled France had failed
Like a brief dream of unremaining glory,
From visions of despair I rose, and scaled
The peak of an aerial promontory,
Whose caverned base with the vexed surge was hoary;
And saw the golden dawn break forth, and waken
Each cloud, and every wave: but transitory
The calm; for sudden, the firm earth was shaken,
As if by the last wreck its frame were overtaken.

2.
So as I stood, one blast of muttering thunder
Burst in far peals along the waveless deep,
When, gathering fast, around, above, and under,
Long trains of tremulous mist began to creep,
Until their complicating lines did steep
The orient sun in shadow: not a sound
Was heard; one horrible repose did keep
The forests and the floods, and all around
Darkness more dread than night was poured upon the ground.

3.
Hark! 'tis the rushing of a wind that sweeps
Earth and the ocean. See! the lightnings yawn
Deluging Heaven with fire, and the lashed deeps
Glitter and boil beneath: it rages on,
One mighty stream, whirlwind and waves upthrown,
Lightning, and hail, and darkness eddying by.
There is a pause, the sea-birds, that were gone
Into their caves to shriek, come forth, to spy
What calm has fall'n on earth, what light is in the sky.

4.
For, where the irresistible storm had cloven

That fearful darkness, the blue sky was seen
Fretted with many a fair cloud interwoven
Most delicately, and the ocean green,
Beneath that opening spot of blue serene,
Quivered like burning emerald; calm was spread
On all below; but far on high, between
Earth and the upper air, the vast clouds fled,
Countless and swift as leaves on autumn's tempest shed.

5.
For ever, as the war became more fierce
Between the whirlwinds and the rack on high,
That spot grew more serene; blue light did pierce
The woof of those white clouds, which seem to lie
Far, deep, and motionless; while through the sky
The pallid semicircle of the moon
Passed on, in slow and moving majesty;
Its upper horn arrayed in mists, which soon
But slowly fled, like dew beneath the beams of noon.

6.
I could not choose but gaze; a fascination
Dwelt in that moon, and sky, and clouds, which drew
My fancy thither, and in expectation
Of what I knew not, I remained: the hue
Of the white moon, amid that heaven so blue,
Suddenly stained with shadow did appear;
A speck, a cloud, a shape, approaching grew,
Like a great ship in the sun's sinking sphere
Beheld afar at sea, and swift it came anear.

7.
Even like a bark, which from a chasm of mountains,
Dark, vast and overhanging, on a river
Which there collects the strength of all its fountains,
Comes forth, whilst with the speed its frame doth quiver,
Sails, oars and stream, tending to one endeavour;
So, from that chasm of light a winged Form
On all the winds of heaven approaching ever
Floated, dilating as it came; the storm
Pursued it with fierce blasts, and lightnings swift and warm.

8.
A course precipitous, of dizzy speed,
Suspending thought and breath; a monstrous sight!
For in the air do I behold indeed
An Eagle and a Serpent wreathed in fight:

And now, relaxing its impetuous flight,
Before the aerial rock on which I stood,
The Eagle, hovering, wheeled to left and right,
And hung with lingering wings over the flood,
And startled with its yells the wide air's solitude.

9.
A shaft of light upon its wings descended,
And every golden feather gleamed therein
Feather and scale, inextricably blended.
The Serpent's mailed and many-coloured skin
Shone through the plumes its coils were twined within
By many a swoln and knotted fold, and high
And far, the neck, receding lithe and thin,
Sustained a crested head, which warily
Shifted and glanced before the Eagle's steadfast eye.

10.
Around, around, in ceaseless circles wheeling
With clang of wings and scream, the Eagle sailed
Incessantly, sometimes on high concealing
Its lessening orbs, sometimes as if it failed,
Drooped through the air; and still it shrieked and wailed,
And casting back its eager head, with beak
And talon unremittingly assailed
The wreathed Serpent, who did ever seek
Upon his enemy's heart a mortal wound to wreak.

11.
What life, what power, was kindled and arose
Within the sphere of that appalling fray!
For, from the encounter of those wondrous foes,
A vapour like the sea's suspended spray
Hung gathered; in the void air, far away,
Floated the shattered plumes; bright scales did leap,
Where'er the Eagle's talons made their way,
Like sparks into the darkness; as they sweep,
Blood stains the snowy foam of the tumultuous deep.

12.
Swift chances in that combat, many a check,
And many a change, a dark and wild turmoil;
Sometimes the Snake around his enemy's neck
Locked in stiff rings his adamantine coil,
Until the Eagle, faint with pain and toil,
Remitted his strong flight, and near the sea
Languidly fluttered, hopeless so to foil

His adversary, who then reared on high
His red and burning crest, radiant with victory.

13.
Then on the white edge of the bursting surge,
Where they had sunk together, would the Snake
Relax his suffocating grasp, and scourge
The wind with his wild writhings; for to break
That chain of torment, the vast bird would shake
The strength of his unconquerable wings
As in despair, and with his sinewy neck,
Dissolve in sudden shock those linked rings
Then soar, as swift as smoke from a volcano springs.

14.
Wile baffled wile, and strength encountered strength,
Thus long, but unprevailing: the event
Of that portentous fight appeared at length:
Until the lamp of day was almost spent
It had endured, when lifeless, stark, and rent,
Hung high that mighty Serpent, and at last
Fell to the sea, while o'er the continent
With clang of wings and scream the Eagle passed,
Heavily borne away on the exhausted blast.

15.
And with it fled the tempest, so that ocean
And earth and sky shone through the atmosphere
Only, 'twas strange to see the red commotion
Of waves like mountains o'er the sinking sphere
Of sunset sweep, and their fierce roar to hear
Amid the calm: down the steep path I wound
To the sea-shore, the evening was most clear
And beautiful, and there the sea I found
Calm as a cradled child in dreamless slumber bound.

16.
There was a Woman, beautiful as morning,
Sitting beneath the rocks, upon the sand
Of the waste sea, fair as one flower adorning
An icy wilderness; each delicate hand
Lay crossed upon her bosom, and the band
Of her dark hair had fall'n, and so she sate
Looking upon the waves; on the bare strand
Upon the sea-mark a small boat did wait,
Fair as herself, like Love by Hope left desolate.

17.
It seemed that this fair Shape had looked upon
That unimaginable fight, and now
That her sweet eyes were weary of the sun,
As brightly it illustrated her woe;
For in the tears which silently to flow
Paused not, its lustre hung: she watching aye
The foam-wreaths which the faint tide wove below
Upon the spangled sands, groaned heavily,
And after every groan looked up over the sea.

18.
And when she saw the wounded Serpent make
His path between the waves, her lips grew pale,
Parted, and quivered; the tears ceased to break
From her immovable eyes; no voice of wail
Escaped her; but she rose, and on the gale
Loosening her star-bright robe and shadowy hair
Poured forth her voice; the caverns of the vale
That opened to the ocean, caught it there,
And filled with silver sounds the overflowing air.

19.
She spake in language whose strange melody
Might not belong to earth. I heard alone,
What made its music more melodious be,
The pity and the love of every tone;
But to the Snake those accents sweet were known
His native tongue and hers; nor did he beat
The hoar spray idly then, but winding on
Through the green shadows of the waves that meet
Near to the shore, did pause beside her snowy feet.

20.
Then on the sands the Woman sate again,
And wept and clasped her hands, and all between,
Renewed the unintelligible strain
Of her melodious voice and eloquent mien;
And she unveiled her bosom, and the green
And glancing shadows of the sea did play
O'er its marmoreal depth: one moment seen,
For ere the next, the Serpent did obey
Her voice, and, coiled in rest in her embrace it lay.

21.
Then she arose, and smiled on me with eyes
Serene yet sorrowing, like that planet fair,

While yet the daylight lingereth in the skies
Which cleaves with arrowy beams the dark-red air,
And said: 'To grieve is wise, but the despair
Was weak and vain which led thee here from sleep:
This shalt thou know, and more, if thou dost dare

With me and with this Serpent, o'er the deep,
A voyage divine and strange, companionship to keep.'

22.
Her voice was like the wildest, saddest tone,
Yet sweet, of some loved voice heard long ago.
I wept. 'Shall this fair woman all alone,
Over the sea with that fierce Serpent go?
His head is on her heart, and who can know
How soon he may devour his feeble prey?'
Such were my thoughts, when the tide gan to flow;
And that strange boat like the moon's shade did sway
Amid reflected stars that in the waters lay:

23.
A boat of rare device, which had no sail
But its own curved prow of thin moonstone,
Wrought like a web of texture fine and frail,
To catch those gentlest winds which are not known
To breathe, but by the steady speed alone
With which it cleaves the sparkling sea; and now
We are embarked, the mountains hang and frown
Over the starry deep that gleams below,
A vast and dim expanse, as o'er the waves we go.

24.
And as we sailed, a strange and awful tale
That Woman told, like such mysterious dream
As makes the slumberer's cheek with wonder pale!
'Twas midnight, and around, a shoreless stream,
Wide ocean rolled, when that majestic theme
Shrined in her heart found utterance, and she bent
Her looks on mine; those eyes a kindling beam
Of love divine into my spirit sent,
And ere her lips could move, made the air eloquent.

25.
'Speak not to me, but hear! Much shalt thou learn,
Much must remain unthought, and more untold,
In the dark Future's ever-flowing urn:
Know then, that from the depth of ages old

Two Powers o'er mortal things dominion hold,
Ruling the world with a divided lot,
Immortal, all-pervading, manifold,
Twin Genii, equal Gods, when life and thought
Sprang forth, they burst the womb of inessential Nought.

26.
'The earliest dweller of the world, alone,
Stood on the verge of chaos. Lo! afar
O'er the wide wild abyss two meteors shone,
Sprung from the depth of its tempestuous jar:
A blood-red Comet and the Morning Star
Mingling their beams in combat as he stood,
All thoughts within his mind waged mutual war,
In dreadful sympathy, when to the flood
That fair Star fell, he turned and shed his brother's blood.

27.
'Thus evil triumphed, and the Spirit of evil,
One Power of many shapes which none may know,
One Shape of many names; the Fiend did revel
In victory, reigning o'er a world of woe,
For the new race of man went to and fro,
Famished and homeless, loathed and loathing, wild,
And hating good for his immortal foe,
He changed from starry shape, beauteous and mild,
To a dire Snake, with man and beast unreconciled.

28.
'The darkness lingering o'er the dawn of things,
Was Evil's breath and life; this made him strong
To soar aloft with overshadowing wings;
And the great Spirit of Good did creep among
The nations of mankind, and every tongue
Cursed and blasphemed him as he passed; for none
Knew good from evil, though their names were hung
In mockery o'er the fane where many a groan,
As King, and Lord, and God, the conquering Fiend did own,

29.
'The Fiend, whose name was Legion: Death, Decay,
Earthquake and Blight, and Want, and Madness pale,
Winged and wan diseases, an array
Numerous as leaves that strew the autumnal gale;
Poison, a snake in flowers, beneath the veil
Of food and mirth, hiding his mortal head;
And, without whom all these might nought avail,

Fear, Hatred, Faith, and Tyranny, who spread
Those subtle nets which snare the living and the dead.

30.
'His spirit is their power, and they his slaves
In air, and light, and thought, and language, dwell;
And keep their state from palaces to graves,
In all resorts of men, invisible,
But when, in ebon mirror, Nightmare fell
To tyrant or impostor bids them rise,
Black winged demon forms, whom, from the hell,
His reign and dwelling beneath nether skies,
He loosens to their dark and blasting ministries.

31.
'In the world's youth his empire was as firm
As its foundations...Soon the Spirit of Good,
Though in the likeness of a loathsome worm,
Sprang from the billows of the formless flood,
Which shrank and fled; and with that Fiend of blood
Renewed the doubtful war...Thrones then first shook,
And earth's immense and trampled multitude
In hope on their own powers began to look,
And Fear, the demon pale, his sanguine shrine forsook.

32.
'Then Greece arose, and to its bards and sages,
In dream, the golden-pinioned Genii came,
Even where they slept amid the night of ages,
Steeping their hearts in the divinest flame
Which thy breath kindled, Power of holiest name!
And oft in cycles since, when darkness gave
New weapons to thy foe, their sunlike fame
Upon the combat shone, a light to save,
Like Paradise spread forth beyond the shadowy grave.

33.
'Such is this conflict when mankind doth strive
With its oppressors in a strife of blood,
Or when free thoughts, like lightnings, are alive,
And in each bosom of the multitude
Justice and truth with Custom's hydra brood
Wage silent war; when Priests and Kings dissemble
In smiles or frowns their fierce disquietude,
When round pure hearts a host of hopes assemble,
The Snake and Eagle meet the world's foundations tremble!

34.
'Thou hast beheld that fight, when to thy home
Thou dost return, steep not its hearth in tears;
Though thou may'st hear that earth is now become
The tyrant's garbage, which to his compeers,
The vile reward of their dishonoured years,
He will dividing give. The victor Fiend,
Omnipotent of yore, now quails, and fears
His triumph dearly won, which soon will lend
An impulse swift and sure to his approaching end.

35.
'List, stranger, list, mine is an human form,
Like that thou wearest, touch me, shrink not now!
My hand thou feel'st is not a ghost's, but warm
With human blood. 'Twas many years ago,
Since first my thirsting soul aspired to know
The secrets of this wondrous world, when deep
My heart was pierced with sympathy, for woe
Which could not be mine own, and thought did keep,
In dream, unnatural watch beside an infant's sleep.

36.
'Woe could not be mine own, since far from men
I dwelt, a free and happy orphan child,
By the sea-shore, in a deep mountain glen;
And near the waves, and through the forests wild,
I roamed, to storm and darkness reconciled:
For I was calm while tempest shook the sky:
But when the breathless heavens in beauty smiled,
I wept, sweet tears, yet too tumultuously
For peace, and clasped my hands aloft in ecstasy.

37.
'These were forebodings of my fate before
A woman's heart beat in my virgin breast,
It had been nurtured in divinest lore:
A dying poet gave me books, and blessed
With wild but holy talk the sweet unrest
In which I watched him as he died away
A youth with hoary hair, a fleeting guest
Of our lone mountains: and this lore did sway
My spirit like a storm, contending there alway.

38.
'Thus the dark tale which history doth unfold
I knew, but not, methinks, as others know,

For they weep not; and Wisdom had unrolled
The clouds which hide the gulf of mortal woe,
To few can she that warning vision show
For I loved all things with intense devotion;
So that when Hope's deep source in fullest flow,
Like earthquake did uplift the stagnant ocean
Of human thoughts, mine shook beneath the wide emotion.

39.
'When first the living blood through all these veins
Kindled a thought in sense, great France sprang forth,
And seized, as if to break, the ponderous chains
Which bind in woe the nations of the earth.
I saw, and started from my cottage-hearth;
And to the clouds and waves in tameless gladness
Shrieked, till they caught immeasurable mirth
And laughed in light and music: soon, sweet madness
Was poured upon my heart, a soft and thrilling sadness.

40.
'Deep slumber fell on me: my dreams were fire
Soft and delightful thoughts did rest and hover
Like shadows o'er my brain; and strange desire,
The tempest of a passion, raging over
My tranquil soul, its depths with light did cover,
Which passed; and calm, and darkness, sweeter far,
Came then I loved; but not a human lover!
For when I rose from sleep, the Morning Star
Shone through the woodbine-wreaths which round my casement were.

41.
''Twas like an eye which seemed to smile on me.
I watched, till by the sun made pale, it sank
Under the billows of the heaving sea;
But from its beams deep love my spirit drank,
And to my brain the boundless world now shrank
Into one thought, one image, yes, forever!
Even like the dayspring, poured on vapours dank,
The beams of that one Star did shoot and quiver
Through my benighted mind and were extinguished never.

42.
'The day passed thus: at night, methought, in dream
A shape of speechless beauty did appear:
It stood like light on a careering stream
Of golden clouds which shook the atmosphere;
A winged youth, his radiant brow did wear

The Morning Star: a wild dissolving bliss
Over my frame he breathed, approaching near,
And bent his eyes of kindling tenderness
Near mine, and on my lips impressed a lingering kiss,

43.
'And said: "A Spirit loves thee, mortal maiden,
How wilt thou prove thy worth?" Then joy and sleep
Together fled; my soul was deeply laden,
And to the shore I went to muse and weep;
But as I moved, over my heart did creep
A joy less soft, but more profound and strong
Than my sweet dream; and it forbade to keep
The path of the sea-shore: that Spirit's tongue
Seemed whispering in my heart, and bore my steps along.

44.
'How, to that vast and peopled city led,
Which was a field of holy warfare then,
I walked among the dying and the dead,
And shared in fearless deeds with evil men,
Calm as an angel in the dragon's den
How I braved death for liberty and truth,
And spurned at peace, and power, and fame and when
Those hopes had lost the glory of their youth,
How sadly I returned, might move the hearer's ruth:

45.
'Warm tears throng fast! the tale may not be said
Know then, that when this grief had been subdued,
I was not left, like others, cold and dead;
The Spirit whom I loved, in solitude
Sustained his child: the tempest-shaken wood,
The waves, the fountains, and the hush of night
These were his voice, and well I understood
His smile divine, when the calm sea was bright
With silent stars, and Heaven was breathless with delight.

46.
'In lonely glens, amid the roar of rivers,
When the dim nights were moonless, have I known
Joys which no tongue can tell; my pale lip quivers
When thought revisits them: know thou alone,
That after many wondrous years were flown,
I was awakened by a shriek of woe;
And over me a mystic robe was thrown,
By viewless hands, and a bright Star did glow

Before my steps the Snake then met his mortal foe.'

47.
'Thou fearest not then the Serpent on thy heart?'
'Fear it!' she said, with brief and passionate cry,
And spake no more: that silence made me start
I looked, and we were sailing pleasantly,
Swift as a cloud between the sea and sky;
Beneath the rising moon seen far away,
Mountains of ice, like sapphire, piled on high,
Hemming the horizon round, in silence lay
On the still waters, these we did approach alway.

48.
And swift and swifter grew the vessel's motion,
So that a dizzy trance fell on my brain
Wild music woke me; we had passed the ocean
Which girds the pole, Nature's remotest reign
And we glode fast o'er a pellucid plain
Of waters, azure with the noontide day.
Ethereal mountains shone around a Fane
Stood in the midst, girt by green isles which lay
On the blue sunny deep, resplendent far away.

49.
It was a Temple, such as mortal hand
Has never built, nor ecstasy, nor dream
Reared in the cities of enchanted land:
'Twas likest Heaven, ere yet day's purple stream
Ebbs o'er the western forest, while the gleam
Of the unrisen moon among the clouds
Is gathering, when with many a golden beam
The thronging constellations rush in crowds,
Paving with fire the sky and the marmoreal floods.

50.
Like what may be conceived of this vast dome,
When from the depths which thought can seldom pierce
Genius beholds it rise, his native home,
Girt by the deserts of the Universe;
Yet, nor in painting's light, or mightier verse,
Or sculpture's marble language, can invest
That shape to mortal sense, such glooms immerse
That incommunicable sight, and rest
Upon the labouring brain and overburdened breast.

51.

Winding among the lawny islands fair,
Whose blosmy forests starred the shadowy deep,
The wingless boat paused where an ivory stair
Its fretwork in the crystal sea did steep,
Encircling that vast Fane's aerial heap:
We disembarked, and through a portal wide
We passed, whose roof of moonstone carved, did keep
A glimmering o'er the forms on every side,
Sculptures like life and thought, immovable, deep-eyed.

52.
We came to a vast hall, whose glorious roof
Was diamond, which had drunk the lightning's sheen
In darkness, and now poured it through the woof

Of spell-inwoven clouds hung there to screen
Its blinding splendour, through such veil was seen
That work of subtlest power, divine and rare;
Orb above orb, with starry shapes between,
And horned moons, and meteors strange and fair,
On night-black columns poised, one hollow hemisphere!

53.
Ten thousand columns in that quivering light
Distinct between whose shafts wound far away
The long and labyrinthine aisles more bright
With their own radiance than the Heaven of Day;
And on the jasper walls around, there lay
Paintings, the poesy of mightiest thought,
Which did the Spirit's history display;
A tale of passionate change, divinely taught,
Which, in their winged dance, unconscious Genii wrought.

54.
Beneath, there sate on many a sapphire throne,
The Great, who had departed from mankind,
A mighty Senate; some, whose white hair shone
Like mountain snow, mild, beautiful, and blind;
Some, female forms, whose gestures beamed with mind;
And ardent youths, and children bright and fair;
And some had lyres whose strings were intertwined
With pale and clinging flames, which ever there
Waked faint yet thrilling sounds that pierced the crystal air.

55.
One seat was vacant in the midst, a throne,
Reared on a pyramid like sculptured flame,

Distinct with circling steps which rested on
Their own deep fire, soon as the Woman came
Into that hall, she shrieked the Spirit's name
And fell; and vanished slowly from the sight.
Darkness arose from her dissolving frame,
Which gathering, filled that dome of woven light,
Blotting its sphered stars with supernatural night.

56.
Then first, two glittering lights were seen to glide
In circles on the amethystine floor,
Small serpent eyes trailing from side to side,
Like meteors on a river's grassy shore,
They round each other rolled, dilating more
And more, then rose, commingling into one,
One clear and mighty planet hanging o'er
A cloud of deepest shadow, which was thrown
Athwart the glowing steps and the crystalline throne.

57.
The cloud which rested on that cone of flame
Was cloven; beneath the planet sate a Form,
Fairer than tongue can speak or thought may frame,
The radiance of whose limbs rose-like and warm
Flowed forth, and did with softest light inform
The shadowy dome, the sculptures, and the state
Of those assembled shapes, with clinging charm
Sinking upon their hearts and mine. He sate
Majestic, yet most mild, calm, yet compassionate.

58.
Wonder and joy a passing faintness threw
Over my brow a hand supported me,
Whose touch was magic strength; an eye of blue
Looked into mine, like moonlight, soothingly;
And a voice said: 'Thou must a listener be
This day, two mighty Spirits now return,
Like birds of calm, from the world's raging sea,
They pour fresh light from Hope's immortal urn;
A tale of human power, despair not, list and learn!

59.
I looked, and lo! one stood forth eloquently.
His eyes were dark and deep, and the clear brow
Which shadowed them was like the morning sky,
The cloudless Heaven of Spring, when in their flow
Through the bright air, the soft winds as they blow

Wake the green world, his gestures did obey
The oracular mind that made his features glow,
And where his curved lips half-open lay,
Passion's divinest stream had made impetuous way.

60.
Beneath the darkness of his outspread hair
He stood thus beautiful; but there was One
Who sate beside him like his shadow there,
And held his hand far lovelier; she was known
To be thus fair, by the few lines alone
Which through her floating locks and gathered cloak,
Glances of soul-dissolving glory, shone:
None else beheld her eyes in him they woke
Memories which found a tongue as thus he silence broke.

CANTO 2.

1.
The starlight smile of children, the sweet looks
Of women, the fair breast from which I fed,
The murmur of the unreposing brooks,
And the green light which, shifting overhead,
Some tangled bower of vines around me shed,
The shells on the sea-sand, and the wild flowers,
The lamp-light through the rafters cheerly spread,
And on the twining flax in life's young hours
These sights and sounds did nurse my spirit's folded powers.

2.
In Argolis, beside the echoing sea,
Such impulses within my mortal frame
Arose, and they were dear to memory,
Like tokens of the dead: but others came
Soon, in another shape: the wondrous fame
Of the past world, the vital words and deeds
Of minds whom neither time nor change can tame,
Traditions dark and old, whence evil creeds
Start forth, and whose dim shade a stream of poison feeds.

3.
I heard, as all have heard, the various story
Of human life, and wept unwilling tears.
Feeble historians of its shame and glory,
False disputants on all its hopes and fears,
Victims who worshipped ruin, chroniclers

Of daily scorn, and slaves who loathed their state
Yet, flattering power, had given its ministers
A throne of judgement in the grave: 'twas fate,
That among such as these my youth should seek its mate.

4.
The land in which I lived, by a fell bane
Was withered up. Tyrants dwelt side by side,
And stabled in our homes, until the chain
Stifled the captive's cry, and to abide
That blasting curse men had no shame, all vied
In evil, slave and despot; fear with lust
Strange fellowship through mutual hate had tied,
Like two dark serpents tangled in the dust,
Which on the paths of men their mingling poison thrust.

5.
Earth, our bright home, its mountains and its waters,
And the ethereal shapes which are suspended
Over its green expanse, and those fair daughters,
The clouds, of Sun and Ocean, who have blended
The colours of the air since first extended
It cradled the young world, none wandered forth
To see or feel; a darkness had descended
On every heart; the light which shows its worth,
Must among gentle thoughts and fearless take its birth.

6.
This vital world, this home of happy spirits,
Was as a dungeon to my blasted kind;
All that despair from murdered hope inherits
They sought, and in their helpless misery blind,
A deeper prison and heavier chains did find,
And stronger tyrants: a dark gulf before,
The realm of a stern Ruler, yawned; behind,
Terror and Time conflicting drove, and bore
On their tempestuous flood the shrieking wretch from shore.

7.
Out of that Ocean's wrecks had Guilt and Woe
Framed a dark dwelling for their homeless thought,
And, starting at the ghosts which to and fro
Glide o'er its dim and gloomy strand, had brought
The worship thence which they each other taught.
Well might men loathe their life, well might they turn
Even to the ills again from which they sought
Such refuge after death! well might they learn

To gaze on this fair world with hopeless unconcern!

8.
For they all pined in bondage; body and soul,
Tyrant and slave, victim and torturer, bent
Before one Power, to which supreme control
Over their will by their own weakness lent,
Made all its many names omnipotent;
All symbols of things evil, all divine;
And hymns of blood or mockery, which rent
The air from all its fanes, did intertwine
Imposture's impious toils round each discordant shrine.

9.
I heard, as all have heard, life's various story,
And in no careless heart transcribed the tale;
But, from the sneers of men who had grown hoary
In shame and scorn, from groans of crowds made pale
By famine, from a mother's desolate wail
O'er her polluted child, from innocent blood
Poured on the earth, and brows anxious and pale
With the heart's warfare, did I gather food
To feed my many thoughts, a tameless multitude!

10.
I wandered through the wrecks of days departed
Far by the desolated shore, when even
O'er the still sea and jagged islets darted
The light of moonrise; in the northern Heaven,
Among the clouds near the horizon driven,
The mountains lay beneath one planet pale;
Around me, broken tombs and columns riven
Looked vast in twilight, and the sorrowing gale
Waked in those ruins gray its everlasting wail!

11.
I knew not who had framed these wonders then,
Nor had I heard the story of their deeds;
But dwellings of a race of mightier men,
And monuments of less ungentle creeds
Tell their own tale to him who wisely heeds
The language which they speak; and now, to me
The moonlight making pale the blooming weeds,
The bright stars shining in the breathless sea,
Interpreted those scrolls of mortal mystery.

12.

Such man has been, and such may yet become!
Ay, wiser, greater, gentler even than they
Who on the fragments of yon shattered dome
Have stamped the sign of power, I felt the sway
Of the vast stream of ages bear away
My floating thoughts, my heart beat loud and fast
Even as a storm let loose beneath the ray
Of the still moon, my spirit onward passed
Beneath truth's steady beams upon its tumult cast.

13.
It shall be thus no more! too long, too long,
Sons of the glorious dead, have ye lain bound
In darkness and in ruin! Hope is strong,
Justice and Truth their winged child have found
Awake! arise! until the mighty sound
Of your career shall scatter in its gust
The thrones of the oppressor, and the ground
Hide the last altar's unregarded dust,
Whose Idol has so long betrayed your impious trust!

14.
It must be so I will arise and waken
The multitude, and like a sulphurous hill,
Which on a sudden from its snows has shaken
The swoon of ages, it shall burst and fill
The world with cleansing fire; it must, it will
It may not be restrained! and who shall stand
Amid the rocking earthquake steadfast still,
But Laon? on high Freedom's desert land
A tower whose marble walls the leagued storms withstand!

15.
One summer night, in commune with the hope
Thus deeply fed, amid those ruins gray
I watched, beneath the dark sky's starry cope;
And ever from that hour upon me lay
The burden of this hope, and night or day,
In vision or in dream, clove to my breast:
Among mankind, or when gone far away
To the lone shores and mountains, 'twas a guest
Which followed where I fled, and watched when I did rest.

16.
These hopes found words through which my spirit sought
To weave a bondage of such sympathy,
As might create some response to the thought

Which ruled me now and as the vapours lie
Bright in the outspread morning's radiancy,
So were these thoughts invested with the light
Of language: and all bosoms made reply
On which its lustre streamed, whene'er it might
Through darkness wide and deep those tranced spirits smite.

17.
Yes, many an eye with dizzy tears was dim,
And oft I thought to clasp my own heart's brother,
When I could feel the listener's senses swim,
And hear his breath its own swift gaspings smother
Even as my words evoked them and another,
And yet another, I did fondly deem,
Felt that we all were sons of one great mother;
And the cold truth such sad reverse did seem
As to awake in grief from some delightful dream.

18.
Yes, oft beside the ruined labyrinth
Which skirts the hoary caves of the green deep,
Did Laon and his friend, on one gray plinth,
Round whose worn base the wild waves hiss and leap,
Resting at eve, a lofty converse keep:
And that this friend was false, may now be said
Calmly that he like other men could weep
Tears which are lies, and could betray and spread
Snares for that guileless heart which for his own had bled.

19.
Then, had no great aim recompensed my sorrow,
I must have sought dark respite from its stress
In dreamless rest, in sleep that sees no morrow
For to tread life's dismaying wilderness
Without one smile to cheer, one voice to bless,
Amid the snares and scoffs of human kind,
Is hard but I betrayed it not, nor less
With love that scorned return sought to unbind
The interwoven clouds which make its wisdom blind.

20.
With deathless minds which leave where they have passed
A path of light, my soul communion knew;
Till from that glorious intercourse, at last,
As from a mine of magic store, I drew
Words which were weapons; round my heart there grew
The adamantine armour of their power;

And from my fancy wings of golden hue
Sprang forth, yet not alone from wisdom's tower,
A minister of truth, these plumes young Laon bore.

21.
An orphan with my parents lived, whose eyes
Were lodestars of delight, which drew me home
When I might wander forth; nor did I prize
Aught human thing beneath Heaven's mighty dome
Beyond this child; so when sad hours were come,
And baffled hope like ice still clung to me,
Since kin were cold, and friends had now become
Heartless and false, I turned from all, to be,
Cythna, the only source of tears and smiles to thee.

22.
What wert thou then? A child most infantine,
Yet wandering far beyond that innocent age
In all but its sweet looks and mien divine;
Even then, methought, with the world's tyrant rage
A patient warfare thy young heart did wage,
When those soft eyes of scarcely conscious thought
Some tale, or thine own fancies, would engage
To overflow with tears, or converse fraught
With passion, o'er their depths its fleeting light had wrought.

23.
She moved upon this earth a shape of brightness,
A power, that from its objects scarcely drew
One impulse of her being in her lightness
Most like some radiant cloud of morning dew,
Which wanders through the waste air's pathless blue,
To nourish some far desert; she did seem
Beside me, gathering beauty as she grew,
Like the bright shade of some immortal dream
Which walks, when tempest sleeps, the wave of life's dark stream.

24.
As mine own shadow was this child to me,
A second self, far dearer and more fair;
Which clothed in undissolving radiancy
All those steep paths which languor and despair
Of human things, had made so dark and bare,
But which I trod alone nor, till bereft
Of friends, and overcome by lonely care,
Knew I what solace for that loss was left,
Though by a bitter wound my trusting heart was cleft.

25.
Once she was dear, now she was all I had
To love in human life this playmate sweet,
This child of twelve years old so she was made
My sole associate, and her willing feet
Wandered with mine where earth and ocean meet,
Beyond the aereal mountains whose vast cells
The unreposing billows ever beat,
Through forests wild and old, and lawny dells
Where boughs of incense droop over the emerald wells.

26.
And warm and light I felt her clasping hand
When twined in mine; she followed where I went,
Through the lone paths of our immortal land.
It had no waste but some memorial lent
Which strung me to my toil, some monument
Vital with mind; then Cythna by my side,
Until the bright and beaming day were spent,
Would rest, with looks entreating to abide,
Too earnest and too sweet ever to be denied.

27.
And soon I could not have refused her, thus
For ever, day and night, we two were ne'er
Parted, but when brief sleep divided us:
And when the pauses of the lulling air
Of noon beside the sea had made a lair
For her soothed senses, in my arms she slept,
And I kept watch over her slumbers there,
While, as the shifting visions over her swept,
Amid her innocent rest by turns she smiled and wept.

28.
And, in the murmur of her dreams was heard
Sometimes the name of Laon: suddenly
She would arise, and, like the secret bird
Whom sunset wakens, fill the shore and sky
With her sweet accents, a wild melody!
Hymns which my soul had woven to Freedom, strong
The source of passion, whence they rose, to be;
Triumphant strains, which, like a spirit's tongue,
To the enchanted waves that child of glory sung

29.
Her white arms lifted through the shadowy stream

Of her loose hair. Oh, excellently great
Seemed to me then my purpose, the vast theme
Of those impassioned songs, when Cythna sate
Amid the calm which rapture doth create
After its tumult, her heart vibrating,
Her spirit o'er the Ocean's floating state
From her deep eyes far wandering, on the wing
Of visions that were mine, beyond its utmost spring!

30.
For, before Cythna loved it, had my song
Peopled with thoughts the boundless universe,
A mighty congregation, which were strong
Where'er they trod the darkness to disperse
The cloud of that unutterable curse
Which clings upon mankind: all things became
Slaves to my holy and heroic verse,
Earth, sea and sky, the planets, life and fame
And fate, or whate'er else binds the world's wondrous frame.

31.
And this beloved child thus felt the sway
Of my conceptions, gathering like a cloud
The very wind on which it rolls away:
Hers too were all my thoughts, ere yet, endowed
With music and with light, their fountains flowed
In poesy; and her still and earnest face,
Pallid with feelings which intensely glowed
Within, was turned on mine with speechless grace,
Watching the hopes which there her heart had learned to trace.

32.
In me, communion with this purest being
Kindled intenser zeal, and made me wise
In knowledge, which, in hers mine own mind seeing,
Left in the human world few mysteries:
How without fear of evil or disguise
Was Cythna! what a spirit strong and mild,
Which death, or pain or peril could despise,
Yet melt in tenderness! what genius wild
Yet mighty, was enclosed within one simple child!

33.
New lore was this old age with its gray hair,
And wrinkled legends of unworthy things,
And icy sneers, is nought: it cannot dare
To burst the chains which life forever flings

On the entangled soul's aspiring wings,
So is it cold and cruel, and is made
The careless slave of that dark power which brings
Evil, like blight, on man, who, still betrayed,
Laughs o'er the grave in which his living hopes are laid.

34.
Nor are the strong and the severe to keep
The empire of the world: thus Cythna taught
Even in the visions of her eloquent sleep,
Unconscious of the power through which she wrought
The woof of such intelligible thought,
As from the tranquil strength which cradled lay
In her smile-peopled rest, my spirit sought
Why the deceiver and the slave has sway
O'er heralds so divine of truth's arising day.

35.
Within that fairest form, the female mind,
Untainted by the poison clouds which rest
On the dark world, a sacred home did find:
But else, from the wide earth's maternal breast,
Victorious Evil, which had dispossessed
All native power, had those fair children torn,
And made them slaves to soothe his vile unrest,
And minister to lust its joys forlorn,
Till they had learned to breathe the atmosphere of scorn.

36.
This misery was but coldly felt, till she
Became my only friend, who had endued
My purpose with a wider sympathy;
Thus, Cythna mourned with me the servitude
In which the half of humankind were mewed
Victims of lust and hate, the slaves of slaves,
She mourned that grace and power were thrown as food
To the hyena lust, who, among graves,
Over his loathed meal, laughing in agony, raves.

37.
And I, still gazing on that glorious child,
Even as these thoughts flushed o'er her: 'Cythna sweet,
Well with the world art thou unreconciled;
Never will peace and human nature meet
Till free and equal man and woman greet
Domestic peace; and ere this power can make
In human hearts its calm and holy seat,

This slavery must be broken' as I spake,
From Cythna's eyes a light of exultation brake.

38.
She replied earnestly: 'It shall be mine,
This task, mine, Laon! thou hast much to gain;
Nor wilt thou at poor Cythna's pride repine,
If she should lead a happy female train
To meet thee over the rejoicing plain,
When myriads at thy call shall throng around
The Golden City.' Then the child did strain
My arm upon her tremulous heart, and wound
Her own about my neck, till some reply she found.

39.
I smiled, and spake not. 'Wherefore dost thou smile
At what I say? Laon, I am not weak,
And, though my cheek might become pale the while,
With thee, if thou desirest, will I seek
Through their array of banded slaves to wreak
Ruin upon the tyrants. I had thought
It was more hard to turn my unpractised cheek
To scorn and shame, and this beloved spot
And thee, O dearest friend, to leave and murmur not.

40.
'Whence came I what I am? Thou, Laon, knowest
How a young child should thus undaunted be;
Methinks, it is a power which thou bestowest,
Through which I seek, by most resembling thee,
So to become most good and great and free;
Yet far beyond this Ocean's utmost roar,
In towers and huts are many like to me,
Who, could they see thine eyes, or feel such lore
As I have learnt from them, like me would fear no more.

41.
'Think'st thou that I shall speak unskilfully,
And none will heed me? I remember now,
How once, a slave in tortures doomed to die,
Was saved, because in accents sweet and low
He sung a song his Judge loved long ago,
As he was led to death. All shall relent
Who hear me, tears, as mine have flowed, shall flow,
Hearts beat as mine now beats, with such intent
As renovates the world; a will omnipotent!

42.
'Yes, I will tread Pride's golden palaces,
Through Penury's roofless huts and squalid cells
Will I descend, where'er in abjectness
Woman with some vile slave her tyrant dwells,
There with the music of thine own sweet spells
Will disenchant the captives, and will pour
For the despairing, from the crystal wells
Of thy deep spirit, reason's mighty lore,
And power shall then abound, and hope arise once more.

43.
'Can man be free if woman be a slave?
Chain one who lives, and breathes this boundless air,
To the corruption of a closed grave!
Can they whose mates are beasts, condemned to bear
Scorn, heavier far than toil or anguish, dare
To trample their oppressors? in their home
Among their babes, thou knowest a curse would wear
The shape of woman hoary Crime would come
Behind, and Fraud rebuild religion's tottering dome.

44.
'I am a child: I would not yet depart.
When I go forth alone, bearing the lamp
Aloft which thou hast kindled in my heart,
Millions of slaves from many a dungeon damp
Shall leap in joy, as the benumbing cramp
Of ages leaves their limbs no ill may harm
Thy Cythna ever, truth its radiant stamp
Has fixed, as an invulnerable charm,
Upon her children's brow, dark Falsehood to disarm.

45.
'Wait yet awhile for the appointed day
Thou wilt depart, and I with tears shall stand
Watching thy dim sail skirt the ocean gray;
Amid the dwellers of this lonely land
I shall remain alone and thy command
Shall then dissolve the world's unquiet trance,
And, multitudinous as the desert sand
Borne on the storm, its millions shall advance,
Thronging round thee, the light of their deliverance.

46.
'Then, like the forests of some pathless mountain,
Which from remotest glens two warring winds

Involve in fire which not the loosened fountain
Of broadest floods might quench, shall all the kinds
Of evil, catch from our uniting minds
The spark which must consume them; Cythna then
Will have cast off the impotence that binds
Her childhood now, and through the paths of men
Will pass, as the charmed bird that haunts the serpent's den.

47.
'We part! O Laon, I must dare nor tremble,
To meet those looks no more! Oh, heavy stroke!
Sweet brother of my soul! can I dissemble
The agony of this thought?' As thus she spoke
The gathered sobs her quivering accents broke,
And in my arms she hid her beating breast.
I remained still for tears, sudden she woke
As one awakes from sleep, and wildly pressed
My bosom, her whole frame impetuously possessed.

48.
'We part to meet again but yon blue waste,
Yon desert wide and deep, holds no recess,
Within whose happy silence, thus embraced
We might survive all ills in one caress:
Nor doth the grave, I fear 'tis passionless
Nor yon cold vacant Heaven: we meet again
Within the minds of men, whose lips shall bless
Our memory, and whose hopes its light retain
When these dissevered bones are trodden in the plain.'

49.
I could not speak, though she had ceased, for now
The fountains of her feeling, swift and deep,
Seemed to suspend the tumult of their flow;
So we arose, and by the starlight steep
Went homeward, neither did we speak nor weep,
But, pale, were calm with passion, thus subdued
Like evening shades that o'er the mountains creep,
We moved towards our home; where, in this mood,
Each from the other sought refuge in solitude.

CANTO 3.

1.
What thoughts had sway o'er Cythna's lonely slumber
That night, I know not; but my own did seem

As if they might ten thousand years outnumber
Of waking life, the visions of a dream
Which hid in one dim gulf the troubled stream
Of mind; a boundless chaos wild and vast,
Whose limits yet were never memory's theme:
And I lay struggling as its whirlwinds passed,
Sometimes for rapture sick, sometimes for pain aghast.

2.
Two hours, whose mighty circle did embrace
More time than might make gray the infant world,
Rolled thus, a weary and tumultuous space:
When the third came, like mist on breezes curled,
From my dim sleep a shadow was unfurled:
Methought, upon the threshold of a cave
I sate with Cythna; drooping briony, pearled
With dew from the wild streamlet's shattered wave,
Hung, where we sate to taste the joys which Nature gave.

3.
We lived a day as we were wont to live,
But Nature had a robe of glory on,
And the bright air o'er every shape did weave
Intenser hues, so that the herbless stone,
The leafless bough among the leaves alone,
Had being clearer than its own could be,
And Cythna's pure and radiant self was shown,
In this strange vision, so divine to me,
That if I loved before, now love was agony.

4.
Morn fled, noon came, evening, then night descended,
And we prolonged calm talk beneath the sphere
Of the calm moon, when suddenly was blended
With our repose a nameless sense of fear;
And from the cave behind I seemed to hear
Sounds gathering upwards! accents incomplete,
And stifled shrieks, and now, more near and near,
A tumult and a rush of thronging feet
The cavern's secret depths beneath the earth did beat.

5.
The scene was changed, and away, away, away!
Through the air and over the sea we sped,
And Cythna in my sheltering bosom lay,
And the winds bore me, through the darkness spread
Around, the gaping earth then vomited

Legions of foul and ghastly shapes, which hung
Upon my flight; and ever, as we fled,
They plucked at Cythna, soon to me then clung
A sense of actual things those monstrous dreams among.

6.
And I lay struggling in the impotence
Of sleep, while outward life had burst its bound,
Though, still deluded, strove the tortured sense
To its dire wanderings to adapt the sound
Which in the light of morn was poured around
Our dwelling; breathless, pale and unaware
I rose, and all the cottage crowded found
With armed men, whose glittering swords were bare,
And whose degraded limbs the tyrant's garb did wear.

7.
And, ere with rapid lips and gathered brow
I could demand the cause a feeble shriek
It was a feeble shriek, faint, far and low,
Arrested me, my mien grew calm and meek,
And grasping a small knife, I went to seek
That voice among the crowd 'twas Cythna's cry!
Beneath most calm resolve did agony wreak
Its whirlwind rage: so I passed quietly
Till I beheld, where bound, that dearest child did lie.

8.
I started to behold her, for delight
And exultation, and a joyance free,
Solemn, serene and lofty, filled the light
Of the calm smile with which she looked on me:
So that I feared some brainless ecstasy,
Wrought from that bitter woe, had wildered her
'Farewell! farewell!' she said, as I drew nigh;
'At first my peace was marred by this strange stir,
Now I am calm as truth, its chosen minister.

9.
'Look not so, Laon say farewell in hope,
These bloody men are but the slaves who bear
Their mistress to her task, it was my scope
The slavery where they drag me now, to share,
And among captives willing chains to wear
Awhile, the rest thou knowest, return, dear friend!
Let our first triumph trample the despair
Which would ensnare us now, for in the end,

In victory or in death our hopes and fears must blend.'

10.
These words had fallen on my unheeding ear,
Whilst I had watched the motions of the crew
With seeming-careless glance; not many were
Around her, for their comrades just withdrew
To guard some other victim, so I drew
My knife, and with one impulse, suddenly
All unaware three of their number slew,
And grasped a fourth by the throat, and with loud cry
My countrymen invoked to death or liberty!

11.
What followed then, I know not for a stroke
On my raised arm and naked head, came down,
Filling my eyes with blood. When I awoke,
I felt that they had bound me in my swoon,
And up a rock which overhangs the town,
By the steep path were bearing me; below,
The plain was filled with slaughter, overthrown
The vineyards and the harvests, and the glow
Of blazing roofs shone far o'er the white Ocean's flow.

12.
Upon that rock a mighty column stood,
Whose capital seemed sculptured in the sky,
Which to the wanderers o'er the solitude
Of distant seas, from ages long gone by,
Had made a landmark; o'er its height to fly
Scarcely the cloud, the vulture, or the blast,
Has power and when the shades of evening lie
On Earth and Ocean, its carved summits cast
The sunken daylight far through the aerial waste.

13.
They bore me to a cavern in the hill
Beneath that column, and unbound me there;
And one did strip me stark; and one did fill
A vessel from the putrid pool; one bare
A lighted torch, and four with friendless care
Guided my steps the cavern-paths along,
Then up a steep and dark and narrow stair
We wound, until the torch's fiery tongue
Amid the gushing day beamless and pallid hung.

14.

They raised me to the platform of the pile,
That column's dizzy height: the grate of brass
Through which they thrust me, open stood the while,
As to its ponderous and suspended mass,
With chains which eat into the flesh, alas!
With brazen links, my naked limbs they bound:
The grate, as they departed to repass,
With horrid clangour fell, and the far sound
Of their retiring steps in the dense gloom was drowned.

15.
The noon was calm and bright: around that column
The overhanging sky and circling sea
Spread forth in silentness profound and solemn
The darkness of brief frenzy cast on me,
So that I knew not my own misery:
The islands and the mountains in the day
Like clouds reposed afar; and I could see
The town among the woods below that lay,
And the dark rocks which bound the bright and glassy bay.

16.
It was so calm, that scarce the feathery weed
Sown by some eagle on the topmost stone
Swayed in the air: so bright, that noon did breed
No shadow in the sky beside mine own
Mine, and the shadow of my chain alone.
Below, the smoke of roofs involved in flame
Rested like night, all else was clearly shown
In that broad glare; yet sound to me none came,
But of the living blood that ran within my frame.

17.
The peace of madness fled, and ah, too soon!
A ship was lying on the sunny main,
Its sails were flagging in the breathless noon
Its shadow lay beyond that sight again
Waked, with its presence, in my tranced brain
The stings of a known sorrow, keen and cold:
I knew that ship bore Cythna o'er the plain
Of waters, to her blighting slavery sold,
And watched it with such thoughts as must remain untold.

18.
I watched until the shades of evening wrapped
Earth like an exhalation then the bark
Moved, for that calm was by the sunset snapped.

It moved a speck upon the Ocean dark:
Soon the wan stars came forth, and I could mark
Its path no more! I sought to close mine eyes,
But like the balls, their lids were stiff and stark;
I would have risen, but ere that I could rise,
My parched skin was split with piercing agonies.

19.
I gnawed my brazen chain, and sought to sever
Its adamantine links, that I might die:
O Liberty! forgive the base endeavour,
Forgive me, if, reserved for victory,
The Champion of thy faith e'er sought to fly.
That starry night, with its clear silence, sent
Tameless resolve which laughed at misery
Into my soul linked remembrance lent
To that such power, to me such a severe content.

20.
To breathe, to be, to hope, or to despair
And die, I questioned not; nor, though the Sun
Its shafts of agony kindling through the air
Moved over me, nor though in evening dun,
Or when the stars their visible courses run,
Or morning, the wide universe was spread
In dreary calmness round me, did I shun
Its presence, nor seek refuge with the dead
From one faint hope whose flower a dropping poison shed.

21.
Two days thus passed, I neither raved nor died
Thirst raged within me, like a scorpion's nest
Built in mine entrails; I had spurned aside
The water-vessel, while despair possessed
My thoughts, and now no drop remained! The uprest
Of the third sun brought hunger but the crust
Which had been left, was to my craving breast
Fuel, not food. I chewed the bitter dust,
And bit my bloodless arm, and licked the brazen rust.

22.
My brain began to fail when the fourth morn
Burst o'er the golden isles a fearful sleep,
Which through the caverns dreary and forlorn
Of the riven soul, sent its foul dreams to sweep
With whirlwind swiftness a fall far and deep,
A gulf, a void, a sense of senselessness

These things dwelt in me, even as shadows keep
Their watch in some dim charnel's loneliness,
A shoreless sea, a sky sunless and planetless!

23.
The forms which peopled this terrific trance
I well remember like a choir of devils,
Around me they involved a giddy dance;
Legions seemed gathering from the misty levels
Of Ocean, to supply those ceaseless revels,
Foul, ceaseless shadows: thought could not divide
The actual world from these entangling evils,
Which so bemocked themselves, that I descried
All shapes like mine own self, hideously multiplied.

24.
The sense of day and night, of false and true,
Was dead within me. Yet two visions burst
That darkness, one, as since that hour I knew,
Was not a phantom of the realms accursed,
Where then my spirit dwelt but of the first
I know not yet, was it a dream or no.
But both, though not distincter, were immersed
In hues which, when through memory's waste they flow,
Make their divided streams more bright and rapid now.

25.
Methought that grate was lifted, and the seven
Who brought me thither four stiff corpses bare,
And from the frieze to the four winds of Heaven
Hung them on high by the entangled hair;
Swarthy were three, the fourth was very fair;
As they retired, the golden moon upsprung,
And eagerly, out in the giddy air,
Leaning that I might eat, I stretched and clung
Over the shapeless depth in which those corpses hung.

26.
A woman's shape, now lank and cold and blue,
The dwelling of the many-coloured worm,
Hung there; the white and hollow cheek I drew
To my dry lips what radiance did inform
Those horny eyes? whose was that withered form?
Alas, alas! it seemed that Cythna's ghost
Laughed in those looks, and that the flesh was warm
Within my teeth! a whirlwind keen as frost
Then in its sinking gulfs my sickening spirit tossed.

27.
Then seemed it that a tameless hurricane
Arose, and bore me in its dark career
Beyond the sun, beyond the stars that wane
On the verge of formless space it languished there,
And dying, left a silence lone and drear,
More horrible than famine: in the deep
The shape of an old man did then appear,
Stately and beautiful; that dreadful sleep
His heavenly smiles dispersed, and I could wake and weep.

28.
And, when the blinding tears had fallen, I saw
That column, and those corpses, and the moon,
And felt the poisonous tooth of hunger gnaw
My vitals, I rejoiced, as if the boon
Of senseless death would be accorded soon;
When from that stony gloom a voice arose,
Solemn and sweet as when low winds attune
The midnight pines; the grate did then unclose,
And on that reverend form the moonlight did repose.

29.
He struck my chains, and gently spake and smiled;
As they were loosened by that Hermit old,
Mine eyes were of their madness half beguiled,
To answer those kind looks; he did enfold
His giant arms around me, to uphold
My wretched frame; my scorched limbs he wound
In linen moist and balmy, and as cold
As dew to drooping leaves; the chain, with sound
Like earthquake, through the chasm of that steep stair did bound,

30.
As, lifting me, it fell! What next I heard,
Were billows leaping on the harbour-bar,
And the shrill sea-wind, whose breath idly stirred
My hair; I looked abroad, and saw a star
Shining beside a sail, and distant far
That mountain and its column, the known mark
Of those who in the wide deep wandering are,
So that I feared some Spirit, fell and dark,
In trance had lain me thus within a fiendish bark.

31.
For now indeed, over the salt sea-billow

I sailed: yet dared not look upon the shape
Of him who ruled the helm, although the pillow
For my light head was hollowed in his lap,
And my bare limbs his mantle did enwrap,
Fearing it was a fiend: at last, he bent
O'er me his aged face; as if to snap
Those dreadful thoughts the gentle grandsire bent,
And to my inmost soul his soothing looks he sent.

32.
A soft and healing potion to my lips
At intervals he raised now looked on high,
To mark if yet the starry giant dips
His zone in the dim sea now cheeringly,
Though he said little, did he speak to me.
'It is a friend beside thee, take good cheer,
Poor victim, thou art now at liberty!'
I joyed as those a human tone to hear,
Who in cells deep and lone have languished many a year.

33.
A dim and feeble joy, whose glimpses oft
Were quenched in a relapse of wildering dreams;
Yet still methought we sailed, until aloft
The stars of night grew pallid, and the beams
Of morn descended on the ocean-streams,
And still that aged man, so grand and mild,
Tended me, even as some sick mother seems
To hang in hope over a dying child,
Till in the azure East darkness again was piled.

34.
And then the night-wind steaming from the shore,
Sent odours dying sweet across the sea,
And the swift boat the little waves which bore,
Were cut by its keen keel, though slantingly;
Soon I could hear the leaves sigh, and could see
The myrtle-blossoms starring the dim grove,
As past the pebbly beach the boat did flee
On sidelong wing, into a silent cove,
Where ebon pines a shade under the starlight wove.

CANTO 4.

1.
The old man took the oars, and soon the bark

Smote on the beach beside a tower of stone;
It was a crumbling heap, whose portal dark
With blooming ivy-trails was overgrown;
Upon whose floor the spangling sands were strown,
And rarest sea-shells, which the eternal flood,
Slave to the mother of the months, had thrown
Within the walls of that gray tower, which stood
A changeling of man's art nursed amid Nature's brood.

2.
When the old man his boat had anchored,
He wound me in his arms with tender care,
And very few, but kindly words he said,
And bore me through the tower adown a stair,
Whose smooth descent some ceaseless step to wear
For many a year had fallen. We came at last
To a small chamber, which with mosses rare
Was tapestried, where me his soft hands placed
Upon a couch of grass and oak-leaves interlaced.

3.
The moon was darting through the lattices
Its yellow light, warm as the beams of day
So warm, that to admit the dewy breeze,
The old man opened them; the moonlight lay
Upon a lake whose waters wove their play
Even to the threshold of that lonely home:
Within was seen in the dim wavering ray
The antique sculptured roof, and many a tome
Whose lore had made that sage all that he had become.

4.
The rock-built barrier of the sea was past,
And I was on the margin of a lake,
A lonely lake, amid the forests vast
And snowy mountains: did my spirit wake
From sleep as many-coloured as the snake
That girds eternity? in life and truth,
Might not my heart its cravings ever slake?
Was Cythna then a dream, and all my youth,
And all its hopes and fears, and all its joy and ruth?

5.
Thus madness came again, a milder madness,
Which darkened nought but time's unquiet flow
With supernatural shades of clinging sadness;
That gentle Hermit, in my helpless woe,

By my sick couch was busy to and fro,
Like a strong spirit ministrant of good:
When I was healed, he led me forth to show
The wonders of his sylvan solitude,
And we together sate by that isle-fretted flood.

6.
He knew his soothing words to weave with skill
From all my madness told; like mine own heart,
Of Cythna would he question me, until
That thrilling name had ceased to make me start,
From his familiar lips it was not art,
Of wisdom and of justice when he spoke
When mid soft looks of pity, there would dart
A glance as keen as is the lightning's stroke
When it doth rive the knots of some ancestral oak.

7.
Thus slowly from my brain the darkness rolled,
My thoughts their due array did re-assume
Through the enchantments of that Hermit old;
Then I bethought me of the glorious doom
Of those who sternly struggle to relume
The lamp of Hope o'er man's bewildered lot,
And, sitting by the waters, in the gloom
Of eve, to that friend's heart I told my thought
That heart which had grown old, but had corrupted not.

8.
That hoary man had spent his livelong age
In converse with the dead, who leave the stamp
Of ever-burning thoughts on many a page,
When they are gone into the senseless damp
Of graves; his spirit thus became a lamp
Of splendour, like to those on which it fed;
Through peopled haunts, the City and the Camp,
Deep thirst for knowledge had his footsteps led,
And all the ways of men among mankind he read.

9.
But custom maketh blind and obdurate
The loftiest hearts; he had beheld the woe
In which mankind was bound, but deemed that fate
Which made them abject, would preserve them so;
And in such faith, some steadfast joy to know,
He sought this cell: but when fame went abroad
That one in Argolis did undergo

Torture for liberty, and that the crowd
High truths from gifted lips had heard and understood;

10.
And that the multitude was gathering wide,
His spirit leaped within his aged frame;
In lonely peace he could no more abide,
But to the land on which the victor's flame
Had fed, my native land, the Hermit came:
Each heart was there a shield, and every tongue
Was as a sword of truth, young Laon's name
Rallied their secret hopes, though tyrants sung
Hymns of triumphant joy our scattered tribes among.

11.
He came to the lone column on the rock,
And with his sweet and mighty eloquence
The hearts of those who watched it did unlock,
And made them melt in tears of penitence.
They gave him entrance free to bear me thence.
'Since this,' the old man said, 'seven years are spent,
While slowly truth on thy benighted sense
Has crept; the hope which wildered it has lent
Meanwhile, to me the power of a sublime intent.

12.
'Yes, from the records of my youthful state,
And from the lore of bards and sages old,
From whatsoe'er my wakened thoughts create
Out of the hopes of thine aspirings bold,
Have I collected language to unfold
Truth to my countrymen; from shore to shore
Doctrines of human power my words have told,
They have been heard, and men aspire to more
Than they have ever gained or ever lost of yore.

13.
'In secret chambers parents read, and weep,
My writings to their babes, no longer blind;
And young men gather when their tyrants sleep,
And vows of faith each to the other bind;
And marriageable maidens, who have pined
With love, till life seemed melting through their look,
A warmer zeal, a nobler hope, now find;
And every bosom thus is rapt and shook,
Like autumn's myriad leaves in one swoln mountain-brook.

14.
'The tyrants of the Golden City tremble
At voices which are heard about the streets;
The ministers of fraud can scarce dissemble
The lies of their own heart, but when one meets
Another at the shrine, he inly weets,
Though he says nothing, that the truth is known;
Murderers are pale upon the judgement-seats,
And gold grows vile even to the wealthy crone,
And laughter fills the Fane, and curses shake the Throne.

15.
'Kind thoughts, and mighty hopes, and gentle deeds
Abound, for fearless love, and the pure law
Of mild equality and peace, succeeds
To faiths which long have held the world in awe,
Bloody and false, and cold: as whirlpools draw
All wrecks of Ocean to their chasm, the sway
Of thy strong genius, Laon, which foresaw
This hope, compels all spirits to obey,
Which round thy secret strength now throng in wide array.

16.
'For I have been thy passive instrument'
(As thus the old man spake, his countenance
Gleamed on me like a spirit's) 'thou hast lent
To me, to all, the power to advance
Towards this unforeseen deliverance
From our ancestral chains ay, thou didst rear
That lamp of hope on high, which time nor chance
Nor change may not extinguish, and my share
Of good, was o'er the world its gathered beams to bear.

17.
'But I, alas! am both unknown and old,
And though the woof of wisdom I know well
To dye in hues of language, I am cold
In seeming, and the hopes which inly dwell,
My manners note that I did long repel;
But Laon's name to the tumultuous throng
Were like the star whose beams the waves compel
And tempests, and his soul-subduing tongue
Were as a lance to quell the mailed crest of wrong.

18.
'Perchance blood need not flow, if thou at length
Wouldst rise, perchance the very slaves would spare

Their brethren and themselves; great is the strength
Of words for lately did a maiden fair,
Who from her childhood has been taught to bear
The Tyrant's heaviest yoke, arise, and make
Her sex the law of truth and freedom hear,
And with these quiet words "for thine own sake
I prithee spare me;" did with ruth so take

19.
'All hearts, that even the torturer who had bound
Her meek calm frame, ere it was yet impaled,
Loosened her, weeping then; nor could be found
One human hand to harm her unassailed
Therefore she walks through the great City, veiled
In virtue's adamantine eloquence,
'Gainst scorn, and death and pain thus trebly mailed,
And blending, in the smiles of that defence,
The Serpent and the Dove, Wisdom and Innocence.

20.
'The wild-eyed women throng around her path:
From their luxurious dungeons, from the dust
Of meaner thralls, from the oppressor's wrath,
Or the caresses of his sated lust
They congregate: in her they put their trust;
The tyrants send their armed slaves to quell
Her power; they, even like a thunder-gust
Caught by some forest, bend beneath the spell
Of that young maiden's speech, and to their chiefs rebel.

21.
'Thus she doth equal laws and justice teach
To woman, outraged and polluted long;
Gathering the sweetest fruit in human reach
For those fair hands now free, while armed wrong
Trembles before her look, though it be strong;
Thousands thus dwell beside her, virgins bright,
And matrons with their babes, a stately throng!
Lovers renew the vows which they did plight
In early faith, and hearts long parted now unite,

22.
'And homeless orphans find a home near her,
And those poor victims of the proud, no less,
Fair wrecks, on whom the smiling world with stir,
Thrusts the redemption of its wickedness:
In squalid huts, and in its palaces

Sits Lust alone, while o'er the land is borne
Her voice, whose awful sweetness doth repress
All evil, and her foes relenting turn,
And cast the vote of love in hope's abandoned urn.

23.
'So in the populous City, a young maiden
Has baffled Havoc of the prey which he
Marks as his own, whene'er with chains o'erladen
Men make them arms to hurl down tyranny,
False arbiter between the bound and free;
And o'er the land, in hamlets and in towns
The multitudes collect tumultuously,
And throng in arms; but tyranny disowns
Their claim, and gathers strength around its trembling thrones.

24.
'Blood soon, although unwillingly, to shed
The free cannot forbear the Queen of Slaves,
The hoodwinked Angel of the blind and dead,
Custom, with iron mace points to the graves
Where her own standard desolately waves
Over the dust of Prophets and of Kings.
Many yet stand in her array "she paves
Her path with human hearts," and o'er it flings
The wildering gloom of her immeasurable wings.

25.
'There is a plain beneath the City's wall,
Bounded by misty mountains, wide and vast,
Millions there lift at Freedom's thrilling call
Ten thousand standards wide, they load the blast
Which bears one sound of many voices past,
And startles on his throne their sceptred foe:
He sits amid his idle pomp aghast,
And that his power hath passed away, doth know
Why pause the victor swords to seal his overthrow?

26.
'The tyrant's guards resistance yet maintain:
Fearless, and fierce, and hard as beasts of blood,
They stand a speck amid the peopled plain;
Carnage and ruin have been made their food
From infancy ill has become their good,
And for its hateful sake their will has wove
The chains which eat their hearts. The multitude
Surrounding them, with words of human love,

Seek from their own decay their stubborn minds to move.

27.
'Over the land is felt a sudden pause,
As night and day those ruthless bands around,
The watch of love is kept: a trance which awes
The thoughts of men with hope; as when the sound
Of whirlwind, whose fierce blasts the waves and clouds confound,
Dies suddenly, the mariner in fear
Feels silence sink upon his heart thus bound,
The conquerors pause, and oh! may freemen ne'er
Clasp the relentless knees of Dread, the murderer!

28.
'If blood be shed, 'tis but a change and choice
Of bonds, from slavery to cowardice
A wretched fall! Uplift thy charmed voice!
Pour on those evil men the love that lies
Hovering within those spirit-soothing eyes
Arise, my friend, farewell!' As thus he spake,
From the green earth lightly I did arise,
As one out of dim dreams that doth awake,
And looked upon the depth of that reposing lake.

29.
I saw my countenance reflected there;
And then my youth fell on me like a wind
Descending on still waters my thin hair
Was prematurely gray, my face was lined
With channels, such as suffering leaves behind,
Not age; my brow was pale, but in my cheek
And lips a flush of gnawing fire did find
Their food and dwelling; though mine eyes might speak
A subtle mind and strong within a frame thus weak.

30.
And though their lustre now was spent and faded,
Yet in my hollow looks and withered mien
The likeness of a shape for which was braided
The brightest woof of genius, still was seen
One who, methought, had gone from the world's scene,
And left it vacant 'twas her lover's face
It might resemble her it once had been
The mirror of her thoughts, and still the grace
Which her mind's shadow cast, left there a lingering trace.

31.

What then was I? She slumbered with the dead.
Glory and joy and peace, had come and gone.
Doth the cloud perish, when the beams are fled
Which steeped its skirts in gold? or, dark and lone,
Doth it not through the paths of night unknown,
On outspread wings of its own wind upborne
Pour rain upon the earth? The stars are shown,
When the cold moon sharpens her silver horn
Under the sea, and make the wide night not forlorn.

32.
Strengthened in heart, yet sad, that aged man
I left, with interchange of looks and tears,
And lingering speech, and to the Camp began
My war. O'er many a mountain-chain which rears
Its hundred crests aloft, my spirit bears
My frame; o'er many a dale and many a moor,
And gaily now meseems serene earth wears
The blosmy spring's star-bright investiture,
A vision which aught sad from sadness might allure.

33.
My powers revived within me, and I went,
As one whom winds waft o'er the bending grass,
Through many a vale of that broad continent.
At night when I reposed, fair dreams did pass
Before my pillow; my own Cythna was,
Not like a child of death, among them ever;
When I arose from rest, a woful mass
That gentlest sleep seemed from my life to sever,
As if the light of youth were not withdrawn forever.

34.
Aye as I went, that maiden who had reared
The torch of Truth afar, of whose high deeds
The Hermit in his pilgrimage had heard,
Haunted my thoughts. Ah, Hope its sickness feeds
With whatsoe'er it finds, or flowers or weeds!
Could she be Cythna? Was that corpse a shade
Such as self-torturing thought from madness breeds?
Why was this hope not torture? Yet it made
A light around my steps which would not ever fade.

CANTO 5.

1.
Over the utmost hill at length I sped,
A snowy steep: the moon was hanging low
Over the Asian mountains, and outspread
The plain, the City, and the Camp below,
Skirted the midnight Ocean's glimmering flow;
The City's moonlit spires and myriad lamps,
Like stars in a sublunar sky did glow,
And fires blazed far amid the scattered camps,
Like springs of flame, which burst where'er swift Earthquake stamps.

2.
All slept but those in watchful arms who stood,
And those who sate tending the beacon's light,
And the few sounds from that vast multitude
Made silence more profound. Oh, what a might
Of human thought was cradled in that night!
How many hearts impenetrably veiled
Beat underneath its shade, what secret fight
Evil and good, in woven passions mailed,
Waged through that silent throng a war that never failed!

3.
And now the Power of Good held victory.
So, through the labyrinth of many a tent,
Among the silent millions who did lie
In innocent sleep, exultingly I went;
The moon had left Heaven desert now, but lent
From eastern morn the first faint lustre showed
An armed youth over his spear he bent
His downward face. 'A friend!' I cried aloud,
And quickly common hopes made freemen understood.

4.
I sate beside him while the morning beam
Crept slowly over Heaven, and talked with him
Of those immortal hopes, a glorious theme!
Which led us forth, until the stars grew dim:
And all the while, methought, his voice did swim
As if it drowned in remembrance were
Of thoughts which make the moist eyes overbrim:
At last, when daylight 'gan to fill the air,
He looked on me, and cried in wonder 'Thou art here!'

5.
Then, suddenly, I knew it was the youth
In whom its earliest hopes my spirit found;

But envious tongues had stained his spotless truth,
And thoughtless pride his love in silence bound,
And shame and sorrow mine in toils had wound,
Whilst he was innocent, and I deluded;
The truth now came upon me, on the ground
Tears of repenting joy, which fast intruded,
Fell fast, and o'er its peace our mingling spirits brooded.

6.
Thus, while with rapid lips and earnest eyes
We talked, a sound of sweeping conflict spread
As from the earth did suddenly arise;
From every tent roused by that clamour dread,
Our bands outsprung and seized their arms we sped
Towards the sound: our tribes were gathering far.
Those sanguine slaves amid ten thousand dead
Stabbed in their sleep, trampled in treacherous war
The gentle hearts whose power their lives had sought to spare.

7.
Like rabid snakes, that sting some gentle child
Who brings them food, when winter false and fair
Allures them forth with its cold smiles, so wild
They rage among the camp; they overbear
The patriot hosts confusion, then despair,
Descends like night when 'Laon!' one did cry;
Like a bright ghost from Heaven that shout did scare
The slaves, and widening through the vaulted sky,
Seemed sent from Earth to Heaven in sign of victory.

8.
In sudden panic those false murderers fled,
Like insect tribes before the northern gale:
But swifter still, our hosts encompassed
Their shattered ranks, and in a craggy vale,
Where even their fierce despair might nought avail,
Hemmed them around! and then revenge and fear
Made the high virtue of the patriots fail:
One pointed on his foe the mortal spear
I rushed before its point, and cried 'Forbear, forbear!'

9.
The spear transfixed my arm that was uplifted
In swift expostulation, and the blood
Gushed round its point: I smiled, and 'Oh! thou gifted
With eloquence which shall not be withstood,
Flow thus!' I cried in joy, 'thou vital flood,

Until my heart be dry, ere thus the cause
For which thou wert aught worthy be subdued
Ah, ye are pale, ye weep, your passions pause,
'Tis well! ye feel the truth of love's benignant laws.

10.
'Soldiers, our brethren and our friends are slain.
Ye murdered them, I think, as they did sleep!
Alas, what have ye done? the slightest pain
Which ye might suffer, there were eyes to weep,
But ye have quenched them there were smiles to steep
Your hearts in balm, but they are lost in woe;
And those whom love did set his watch to keep
Around your tents, truth's freedom to bestow,
Ye stabbed as they did sleep but they forgive ye now.

11.
'Oh wherefore should ill ever flow from ill,
And pain still keener pain for ever breed?
We all are brethren even the slaves who kill
For hire, are men; and to avenge misdeed
On the misdoer, doth but Misery feed
With her own broken heart! O Earth, O Heaven!
And thou, dread Nature, which to every deed
And all that lives, or is, to be hath given,
Even as to thee have these done ill, and are forgiven!

12.
'Join then your hands and hearts, and let the past
Be as a grave which gives not up its dead
To evil thoughts.' A film then overcast
My sense with dimness, for the wound, which bled
Freshly, swift shadows o'er mine eyes had shed.
When I awoke, I lay mid friends and foes,
And earnest countenances on me shed
The light of questioning looks, whilst one did close
My wound with balmiest herbs, and soothed me to repose;

13.
And one whose spear had pierced me, leaned beside
With quivering lips and humid eyes; and all
Seemed like some brothers on a journey wide
Gone forth, whom now strange meeting did befall
In a strange land, round one whom they might call
Their friend, their chief, their father, for assay
Of peril, which had saved them from the thrall
Of death, now suffering. Thus the vast array

Of those fraternal bands were reconciled that day.

14.
Lifting the thunder of their acclamation,
Towards the City then the multitude,
And I among them, went in joy a nation
Made free by love; a mighty brotherhood
Linked by a jealous interchange of good;
A glorious pageant, more magnificent
Than kingly slaves arrayed in gold and blood,
When they return from carnage, and are sent
In triumph bright beneath the populous battlement.

15.
Afar, the city-walls were thronged on high,
And myriads on each giddy turret clung,
And to each spire far lessening in the sky
Bright pennons on the idle winds were hung;
As we approached, a shout of joyance sprung
At once from all the crowd, as if the vast
And peopled Earth its boundless skies among
The sudden clamour of delight had cast,
When from before its face some general wreck had passed.

16.
Our armies through the City's hundred gates
Were poured, like brooks which to the rocky lair
Of some deep lake, whose silence them awaits,
Throng from the mountains when the storms are there
And, as we passed through the calm sunny air
A thousand flower-inwoven crowns were shed,
The token flowers of truth and freedom fair,
And fairest hands bound them on many a head,
Those angels of love's heaven that over all was spread.

17.
I trod as one tranced in some rapturous vision:
Those bloody bands so lately reconciled,
Were, ever as they went, by the contrition
Of anger turned to love, from ill beguiled,
And every one on them more gently smiled,
Because they had done evil: the sweet awe
Of such mild looks made their own hearts grow mild,
And did with soft attraction ever draw
Their spirits to the love of freedom's equal law.

18.

And they, and all, in one loud symphony
My name with Liberty commingling, lifted,
'The friend and the preserver of the free!
The parent of this joy!' and fair eyes gifted
With feelings, caught from one who had uplifted
The light of a great spirit, round me shone;
And all the shapes of this grand scenery shifted
Like restless clouds before the steadfast sun,
Where was that Maid? I asked, but it was known of none.

19.
Laone was the name her love had chosen,
For she was nameless, and her birth none knew:
Where was Laone now? The words were frozen
Within my lips with fear; but to subdue
Such dreadful hope, to my great task was due,
And when at length one brought reply, that she
To-morrow would appear, I then withdrew
To judge what need for that great throng might be,
For now the stars came thick over the twilight sea.

20.
Yet need was none for rest or food to care,
Even though that multitude was passing great,
Since each one for the other did prepare
All kindly succour. Therefore to the gate
Of the Imperial House, now desolate,
I passed, and there was found aghast, alone,
The fallen Tyrant! Silently he sate
Upon the footstool of his golden throne,
Which, starred with sunny gems, in its own lustre shone.

21.
Alone, but for one child, who led before him
A graceful dance: the only living thing
Of all the crowd, which thither to adore him
Flocked yesterday, who solace sought to bring
In his abandonment! She knew the King
Had praised her dance of yore, and now she wove
Its circles, aye weeping and murmuring
Mid her sad task of unregarded love,
That to no smiles it might his speechless sadness move.

22.
She fled to him, and wildly clasped his feet
When human steps were heard: he moved nor spoke,
Nor changed his hue, nor raised his looks to meet

The gaze of strangers our loud entrance woke
The echoes of the hall, which circling broke
The calm of its recesses, like a tomb
Its sculptured walls vacantly to the stroke
Of footfalls answered, and the twilight's gloom
Lay like a charnel's mist within the radiant dome.

23.
The little child stood up when we came nigh;
Her lips and cheeks seemed very pale and wan,
But on her forehead, and within her eye
Lay beauty, which makes hearts that feed thereon
Sick with excess of sweetness; on the throne
She leaned; the King, with gathered brow, and lips
Wreathed by long scorn, did inly sneer and frown
With hue like that when some great painter dips
His pencil in the gloom of earthquake and eclipse.

24.
She stood beside him like a rainbow braided
Within some storm, when scarce its shadows vast
From the blue paths of the swift sun have faded;
A sweet and solemn smile, like Cythna's, cast
One moment's light, which made my heart beat fast,
O'er that child's parted lips a gleam of bliss,
A shade of vanished days, as the tears passed
Which wrapped it, even as with a father's kiss
I pressed those softest eyes in trembling tenderness.

25.
The sceptred wretch then from that solitude
I drew, and, of his change compassionate,
With words of sadness soothed his rugged mood.
But he, while pride and fear held deep debate,
With sullen guile of ill-dissembled hate
Glared on me as a toothless snake might glare:
Pity, not scorn I felt, though desolate
The desolator now, and unaware
The curses which he mocked had caught him by the hair.

26.
I led him forth from that which now might seem
A gorgeous grave: through portals sculptured deep
With imagery beautiful as dream
We went, and left the shades which tend on sleep
Over its unregarded gold to keep
Their silent watch. The child trod faintingly,

And as she went, the tears which she did weep
Glanced in the starlight; wildered seemed she,
And, when I spake, for sobs she could not answer me.

27.
At last the tyrant cried, 'She hungers, slave!
Stab her, or give her bread!' It was a tone
Such as sick fancies in a new-made grave
Might hear. I trembled, for the truth was known;
He with this child had thus been left alone,
And neither had gone forth for food, but he
In mingled pride and awe cowered near his throne,
And she a nursling of captivity
Knew nought beyond those walls, nor what such change might be.

28.
And he was troubled at a charm withdrawn
Thus suddenly; that sceptres ruled no more
That even from gold the dreadful strength was gone,
Which once made all things subject to its power
Such wonder seized him, as if hour by hour
The past had come again; and the swift fall
Of one so great and terrible of yore,
To desolateness, in the hearts of all
Like wonder stirred, who saw such awful change befall.

29.
A mighty crowd, such as the wide land pours
Once in a thousand years, now gathered round
The fallen tyrant; like the rush of showers
Of hail in spring, pattering along the ground,
Their many footsteps fell, else came no sound
From the wide multitude: that lonely man
Then knew the burden of his change, and found,
Concealing in the dust his visage wan,
Refuge from the keen looks which through his bosom ran.

30.
And he was faint withal: I sate beside him
Upon the earth, and took that child so fair
From his weak arms, that ill might none betide him
Or her; when food was brought to them, her share
To his averted lips the child did bear,
But, when she saw he had enough, she ate
And wept the while; the lonely man's despair
Hunger then overcame, and of his state
Forgetful, on the dust as in a trance he sate.

31.
Slowly the silence of the multitudes
Passed, as when far is heard in some lone dell
The gathering of a wind among the woods
'And he is fallen!' they cry, 'he who did dwell
Like famine or the plague, or aught more fell
Among our homes, is fallen! the murderer
Who slaked his thirsting soul as from a well
Of blood and tears with ruin! he is here!
Sunk in a gulf of scorn from which none may him rear!'

32.
Then was heard 'He who judged let him be brought
To judgement! blood for blood cries from the soil
On which his crimes have deep pollution wrought!
Shall Othman only unavenged despoil?
Shall they who by the stress of grinding toil
Wrest from the unwilling earth his luxuries,
Perish for crime, while his foul blood may boil,
Or creep within his veins at will? Arise!
And to high justice make her chosen sacrifice!'

33.
'What do ye seek? what fear ye,' then I cried,
Suddenly starting forth, 'that ye should shed
The blood of Othman? if your hearts are tried
In the true love of freedom, cease to dread
This one poor lonely man beneath Heaven spread
In purest light above us all, through earth
Maternal earth, who doth her sweet smiles shed
For all, let him go free; until the worth
Of human nature win from these a second birth.

34.
'What call ye "justice"? Is there one who ne'er
In secret thought has wished another's ill?
Are ye all pure? Let those stand forth who hear
And tremble not. Shall they insult and kill,
If such they be? their mild eyes can they fill
With the false anger of the hypocrite?
Alas, such were not pure! the chastened will
Of virtue sees that justice is the light
Of love, and not revenge, and terror and despite.'

35.
The murmur of the people, slowly dying,

Paused as I spake, then those who near me were,
Cast gentle looks where the lone man was lying
Shrouding his head, which now that infant fair
Clasped on her lap in silence; through the air
Sobs were then heard, and many kissed my feet
In pity's madness, and to the despair
Of him whom late they cursed, a solace sweet
His very victims brought soft looks and speeches meet.

36.
Then to a home for his repose assigned,
Accompanied by the still throng, he went
In silence, where, to soothe his rankling mind,
Some likeness of his ancient state was lent;
And if his heart could have been innocent
As those who pardoned him, he might have ended
His days in peace; but his straight lips were bent,
Men said, into a smile which guile portended,
A sight with which that child like hope with fear was blended.

37.
'Twas midnight now, the eve of that great day
Whereon the many nations at whose call
The chains of earth like mist melted away,
Decreed to hold a sacred Festival,
A rite to attest the equality of all
Who live. So to their homes, to dream or wake
All went. The sleepless silence did recall
Laone to my thoughts, with hopes that make
The flood recede from which their thirst they seek to slake.

38.
The dawn flowed forth, and from its purple fountains
I drank those hopes which make the spirit quail,
As to the plain between the misty mountains
And the great City, with a countenance pale,
I went: it was a sight which might avail
To make men weep exulting tears, for whom
Now first from human power the reverend veil
Was torn, to see Earth from her general womb
Pour forth her swarming sons to a fraternal doom:

39.
To see, far glancing in the misty morning,
The signs of that innumerable host;
To hear one sound of many made, the warning
Of Earth to Heaven from its free children tossed,

While the eternal hills, and the sea lost
In wavering light, and, starring the blue sky
The city's myriad spires of gold, almost
With human joy made mute society
Its witnesses with men who must hereafter be.

40.
To see, like some vast island from the Ocean,
The Altar of the Federation rear
Its pile i' the midst; a work, which the devotion
Of millions in one night created there,
Sudden as when the moonrise makes appear
Strange clouds in the east; a marble pyramid
Distinct with steps: that mighty shape did wear
The light of genius; its still shadow hid
Far ships: to know its height the morning mists forbid!

41.
To hear the restless multitudes for ever
Around the base of that great Altar flow,
As on some mountain-islet burst and shiver
Atlantic waves; and solemnly and slow
As the wind bore that tumult to and fro,
To feel the dreamlike music, which did swim
Like beams through floating clouds on waves below
Falling in pauses, from that Altar dim,
As silver-sounding tongues breathed an aerial hymn.

42.
To hear, to see, to live, was on that morn
Lethean joy! so that all those assembled
Cast off their memories of the past outworn;
Two only bosoms with their own life trembled,
And mine was one, and we had both dissembled;
So with a beating heart I went, and one,
Who having much, covets yet more, resembled;
A lost and dear possession, which not won,
He walks in lonely gloom beneath the noonday sun.

43.
To the great Pyramid I came: its stair
With female choirs was thronged: the loveliest
Among the free, grouped with its sculptures rare;
As I approached, the morning's golden mist,
Which now the wonder-stricken breezes kissed
With their cold lips, fled, and the summit shone
Like Athos seen from Samothracia, dressed

In earliest light, by vintagers, and one
Sate there, a female Shape upon an ivory throne:

44.
A Form most like the imagined habitant
Of silver exhalations sprung from dawn,
By winds which feed on sunrise woven, to enchant
The faiths of men: all mortal eyes were drawn,
As famished mariners through strange seas gone
Gaze on a burning watch-tower, by the light
Of those divinest lineaments alone
With thoughts which none could share, from that fair sight
I turned in sickness, for a veil shrouded her countenance bright.

45.
And neither did I hear the acclamations,
Which from brief silence bursting, filled the air
With her strange name and mine, from all the nations
Which we, they said, in strength had gathered there
From the sleep of bondage; nor the vision fair
Of that bright pageantry beheld, but blind
And silent, as a breathing corpse did fare,
Leaning upon my friend, till like a wind
To fevered cheeks, a voice flowed o'er my troubled mind.

46.
Like music of some minstrel heavenly gifted,
To one whom fiends enthral, this voice to me;
Scarce did I wish her veil to be uplifted,
I was so calm and joyous. I could see
The platform where we stood, the statues three
Which kept their marble watch on that high shrine,
The multitudes, the mountains, and the sea;
As when eclipse hath passed, things sudden shine
To men's astonished eyes most clear and crystalline.

47.
At first Laone spoke most tremulously:
But soon her voice the calmness which it shed
Gathered, and 'Thou art whom I sought to see,
And thou art our first votary here,' she said:
'I had a dear friend once, but he is dead!
And of all those on the wide earth who breathe,
Thou dost resemble him alone I spread
This veil between us two that thou beneath
Shouldst image one who may have been long lost in death.

48.
'For this wilt thou not henceforth pardon me?
Yes, but those joys which silence well requite
Forbid reply; why men have chosen me
To be the Priestess of this holiest rite
I scarcely know, but that the floods of light
Which flow over the world, have borne me hither
To meet thee, long most dear; and now unite
Thine hand with mine, and may all comfort wither
From both the hearts whose pulse in joy now beat together,

49.
'If our own will as others' law we bind,
If the foul worship trampled here we fear;
If as ourselves we cease to love our kind!'
She paused, and pointed upwards sculptured there
Three shapes around her ivory throne appear;
One was a Giant, like a child asleep
On a loose rock, whose grasp crushed, as it were
In dream, sceptres and crowns; and one did keep
Its watchful eyes in doubt whether to smile or weep;

50.
A Woman sitting on the sculptured disk
Of the broad earth, and feeding from one breast
A human babe and a young basilisk;
Her looks were sweet as Heaven's when loveliest
In Autumn eves. The third Image was dressed
In white wings swift as clouds in winter skies;
Beneath his feet, 'mongst ghastliest forms, repressed
Lay Faith, an obscene worm, who sought to rise,
While calmly on the Sun he turned his diamond eyes.

51.
Beside that Image then I sate, while she
Stood, mid the throngs which ever ebbed and flowed,
Like light amid the shadows of the sea
Cast from one cloudless star, and on the crowd
That touch which none who feels forgets, bestowed;
And whilst the sun returned the steadfast gaze
Of the great Image, as o'er Heaven it glode,
That rite had place; it ceased when sunset's blaze
Burned o'er the isles. All stood in joy and deep amaze
When in the silence of all spirits there
Laone's voice was felt, and through the air
Her thrilling gestures spoke, most eloquently fair:

51.1.
'Calm art thou as yon sunset! swift and strong
As new-fledged Eagles, beautiful and young,
That float among the blinding beams of morning;
And underneath thy feet writhe Faith, and Folly,
Custom, and Hell, and mortal Melancholy
Hark! the Earth starts to hear the mighty warning
Of thy voice sublime and holy;
Its free spirits here assembled
See thee, feel thee, know thee now,
To thy voice their hearts have trembled
Like ten thousand clouds which flow
With one wide wind as it flies!
Wisdom! thy irresistible children rise
To hail thee, and the elements they chain
And their own will, to swell the glory of thy train.

51.2.
'O Spirit vast and deep as Night and Heaven!
Mother and soul of all to which is given
The light of life, the loveliness of being,
Lo! thou dost re-ascend the human heart,
Thy throne of power, almighty as thou wert
In dreams of Poets old grown pale by seeing
The shade of thee; now, millions start
To feel thy lightnings through them burning:
Nature, or God, or Love, or Pleasure,
Or Sympathy the sad tears turning
To mutual smiles, a drainless treasure,
Descends amidst us; Scorn and Hate,
Revenge and Selfishness are desolate
A hundred nations swear that there shall be
Pity and Peace and Love, among the good and free!

51.3.
'Eldest of things, divine Equality!
Wisdom and Love are but the slaves of thee,
The Angels of thy sway, who pour around thee
Treasures from all the cells of human thought,
And from the Stars, and from the Ocean brought,
And the last living heart whose beatings bound thee:
The powerful and the wise had sought
Thy coming, thou in light descending
O'er the wide land which is thine own
Like the Spring whose breath is blending
All blasts of fragrance into one,
Comest upon the paths of men!

Earth bares her general bosom to thy ken,
And all her children here in glory meet
To feed upon thy smiles, and clasp thy sacred feet.

51.4
'My brethren, we are free! the plains and mountains,
The gray sea-shore, the forests and the fountains,
Are haunts of happiest dwellers; man and woman,
Their common bondage burst, may freely borrow
From lawless love a solace for their sorrow;
For oft we still must weep, since we are human.
A stormy night's serenest morrow,
Whose showers are pity's gentle tears,
Whose clouds are smiles of those that die
Like infants without hopes or fears,
And whose beams are joys that lie
In blended hearts, now holds dominion;
The dawn of mind, which upwards on a pinion
Borne, swift as sunrise, far illumines space,
And clasps this barren world in its own bright embrace!

51.5
'My brethren, we are free! The fruits are glowing
Beneath the stars, and the night-winds are flowing
O'er the ripe corn, the birds and beasts are dreaming
Never again may blood of bird or beast
Stain with its venomous stream a human feast,
To the pure skies in accusation steaming;
Avenging poisons shall have ceased
To feed disease and fear and madness,
The dwellers of the earth and air
Shall throng around our steps in gladness,
Seeking their food or refuge there.
Our toil from thought all glorious forms shall cull,
To make this Earth, our home, more beautiful,
And Science, and her sister Poesy,
Shall clothe in light the fields and cities of the free!

51.6
'Victory, Victory to the prostrate nations!
Bear witness Night, and ye mute Constellations
Who gaze on us from your crystalline cars!
Thoughts have gone forth whose powers can sleep no more!
Victory! Victory! Earth's remotest shore,
Regions which groan beneath the Antarctic stars,
The green lands cradled in the roar
Of western waves, and wildernesses

Peopled and vast, which skirt the oceans
Where morning dyes her golden tresses,
Shall soon partake our high emotions:
Kings shall turn pale! Almighty Fear,
The Fiend-God, when our charmed name he hear,
Shall fade like shadow from his thousand fanes,
While Truth with Joy enthroned o'er his lost empire reigns!'

51.52.
Ere she had ceased, the mists of night entwining
Their dim woof, floated o'er the infinite throng;
She, like a spirit through the darkness shining,
In tones whose sweetness silence did prolong,
As if to lingering winds they did belong,
Poured forth her inmost soul: a passionate speech
With wild and thrilling pauses woven among,
Which whoso heard was mute, for it could teach
To rapture like her own all listening hearts to reach.

53.
Her voice was as a mountain stream which sweeps
The withered leaves of Autumn to the lake,
And in some deep and narrow bay then sleeps
In the shadow of the shores; as dead leaves wake,
Under the wave, in flowers and herbs which make
Those green depths beautiful when skies are blue,
The multitude so moveless did partake
Such living change, and kindling murmurs flew
As o'er that speechless calm delight and wonder grew.

54.
Over the plain the throngs were scattered then
In groups around the fires, which from the sea
Even to the gorge of the first mountain-glen
Blazed wide and far: the banquet of the free
Was spread beneath many a dark cypress-tree,
Beneath whose spires, which swayed in the red flame,
Reclining, as they ate, of Liberty,
And Hope, and Justice, and Laone's name,
Earth's children did a woof of happy converse frame.

55.
Their feast was such as Earth, the general mother,
Pours from her fairest bosom, when she smiles
In the embrace of Autumn; to each other
As when some parent fondly reconciles
Her warring children, she their wrath beguiles

With her own sustenance, they relenting weep:
Such was this Festival, which from their isles
And continents, and winds, and oceans deep,
All shapes might throng to share, that fly, or walk or creep,

56.
Might share in peace and innocence, for gore
Or poison none this festal did pollute,
But, piled on high, an overflowing store
Of pomegranates and citrons, fairest fruit,
Melons, and dates, and figs, and many a root
Sweet and sustaining, and bright grapes ere yet
Accursed fire their mild juice could transmute
Into a mortal bane, and brown corn set
In baskets; with pure streams their thirsting lips they wet.

57.
Laone had descended from the shrine,
And every deepest look and holiest mind
Fed on her form, though now those tones divine
Were silent as she passed; she did unwind
Her veil, as with the crowds of her own kind
She mixed; some impulse made my heart refrain
From seeking her that night, so I reclined
Amidst a group, where on the utmost plain
A festal watchfire burned beside the dusky main.

58.
And joyous was our feast; pathetic talk,
And wit, and harmony of choral strains,
While far Orion o'er the waves did walk
That flow among the isles, held us in chains
Of sweet captivity which none disdains
Who feels; but when his zone grew dim in mist
Which clothes the Ocean's bosom, o'er the plains
The multitudes went homeward, to their rest,
Which that delightful day with its own shadow blessed.

CANTO 6.

1.
Beside the dimness of the glimmering sea,
Weaving swift language from impassioned themes,
With that dear friend I lingered, who to me
So late had been restored, beneath the gleams

Of the silver stars; and ever in soft dreams
Of future love and peace sweet converse lapped
Our willing fancies, till the pallid beams
Of the last watchfire fell, and darkness wrapped
The waves, and each bright chain of floating fire was snapped;

2.
And till we came even to the City's wall
And the great gate; then, none knew whence or why,
Disquiet on the multitudes did fall:
And first, one pale and breathless passed us by,
And stared and spoke not; then with piercing cry
A troop of wild-eyed women, by the shrieks
Of their own terror driven, tumultuously
Hither and thither hurrying with pale cheeks,
Each one from fear unknown a sudden refuge seeks

3.
Then, rallying cries of treason and of danger
Resounded: and 'They come! to arms! to arms!
The Tyrant is amongst us, and the stranger
Comes to enslave us in his name! to arms!'
In vain: for Panic, the pale fiend who charms
Strength to forswear her right, those millions swept
Like waves before the tempest these alarms
Came to me, as to know their cause I lept
On the gate's turret, and in rage and grief and scorn I wept!

4.
For to the North I saw the town on fire,
And its red light made morning pallid now,
Which burst over wide Asia; louder, higher,
The yells of victory and the screams of woe
I heard approach, and saw the throng below
Stream through the gates like foam-wrought waterfalls
Fed from a thousand storms the fearful glow
Of bombs flares overhead at intervals
The red artillery's bolt mangling among them falls.

5.
And now the horsemen come and all was done
Swifter than I have spoken I beheld
Their red swords flash in the unrisen sun.
I rushed among the rout, to have repelled
That miserable flight one moment quelled
By voice and looks and eloquent despair,
As if reproach from their own hearts withheld

Their steps, they stood; but soon came pouring there
New multitudes, and did those rallied bands o'erbear.

6.
I strove, as, drifted on some cataract
By irresistible streams, some wretch might strive
Who hears its fatal roar: the files compact
Whelmed me, and from the gate availed to drive
With quickening impulse, as each bolt did rive
Their ranks with bloodier chasm: into the plain
Disgorged at length the dead and the alive
In one dread mass, were parted, and the stain
Of blood, from mortal steel fell o'er the fields like rain.

7.
For now the despot's bloodhounds with their prey
Unarmed and unaware, were gorging deep
Their gluttony of death; the loose array
Of horsemen o'er the wide fields murdering sweep,
And with loud laughter for their tyrant reap
A harvest sown with other hopes; the while,
Far overhead, ships from Propontis keep
A killing rain of fire: when the waves smile
As sudden earthquakes light many a volcano-isle,

8.
Thus sudden, unexpected feast was spread
For the carrion-fowls of Heaven. I saw the sight
I moved, I lived, as o'er the heaps of dead,
Whose stony eyes glared in the morning light
I trod; to me there came no thought of flight,
But with loud cries of scorn, which whoso heard
That dreaded death, felt in his veins the might
Of virtuous shame return, the crowd I stirred,
And desperation's hope in many hearts recurred.

9.
A band of brothers gathering round me, made,
Although unarmed, a steadfast front, and still
Retreating, with stern looks beneath the shade
Of gathered eyebrows, did the victors fill
With doubt even in success; deliberate will
Inspired our growing troop; not overthrown
It gained the shelter of a grassy hill,
And ever still our comrades were hewn down,
And their defenceless limbs beneath our footsteps strown.

10.
Immovably we stood in joy I found,
Beside me then, firm as a giant pine
Among the mountain-vapours driven around,
The old man whom I loved his eyes divine
With a mild look of courage answered mine,
And my young friend was near, and ardently
His hand grasped mine a moment now the line
Of war extended, to our rallying cry
As myriads flocked in love and brotherhood to die.

11.
For ever while the sun was climbing Heaven
The horseman hewed our unarmed myriads down
Safely, though when by thirst of carnage driven
Too near, those slaves were swiftly overthrown
By hundreds leaping on them: flesh and bone
Soon made our ghastly ramparts; then the shaft
Of the artillery from the sea was thrown
More fast and fiery, and the conquerors laughed
In pride to hear the wind our screams of torment waft.

12.
For on one side alone the hill gave shelter,
So vast that phalanx of unconquered men,
And there the living in the blood did welter
Of the dead and dying, which in that green glen,
Like stifled torrents, made a plashy fen
Under the feet thus was the butchery waged
While the sun clomb Heaven's eastern steep but when
It 'gan to sink a fiercer combat raged,
For in more doubtful strife the armies were engaged.

13.
Within a cave upon the hill were found
A bundle of rude pikes, the instrument
Of those who war but on their native ground
For natural rights: a shout of joyance sent
Even from our hearts the wide air pierced and rent,
As those few arms the bravest and the best
Seized, and each sixth, thus armed, did now present
A line which covered and sustained the rest,
A confident phalanx, which the foes on every side invest.

14.
That onset turned the foes to flight almost;
But soon they saw their present strength, and knew

That coming night would to our resolute host
Bring victory; so dismounting, close they drew
Their glittering files, and then the combat grew
Unequal but most horrible; and ever
Our myriads, whom the swift bolt overthrew,
Or the red sword, failed like a mountain river
Which rushes forth in foam to sink in sands forever.

15.
Sorrow and shame, to see with their own kind
Our human brethren mix, like beasts of blood,
To mutual ruin armed by one behind
Who sits and scoffs! That friend so mild and good,
Who like its shadow near my youth had stood,
Was stabbed! my old preserver's hoary hair
With the flesh clinging to its roots, was strewed
Under my feet! I lost all sense or care,
And like the rest I grew desperate and unaware.

16.
The battle became ghastlier in the midst
I paused, and saw, how ugly and how fell
O Hate! thou art, even when thy life thou shedd'st
For love. The ground in many a little dell
Was broken, up and down whose steeps befell
Alternate victory and defeat, and there
The combatants with rage most horrible
Strove, and their eyes started with cracking stare,
And impotent their tongues they lolled into the air,

17.
Flaccid and foamy, like a mad dog's hanging;
Want, and Moon-madness, and the pest's swift Bane
When its shafts smite, while yet its bow is twanging
Have each their mark and sign, some ghastly stain;
And this was thine, O War! of hate and pain
Thou loathed slave! I saw all shapes of death
And ministered to many, o'er the plain
While carnage in the sunbeam's warmth did seethe,
Till twilight o'er the east wove her serenest wreath.

18.
The few who yet survived, resolute and firm
Around me fought. At the decline of day
Winding above the mountain's snowy term
New banners shone; they quivered in the ray
Of the sun's unseen orb, ere night the array

Of fresh troops hemmed us in of those brave bands
I soon survived alone and now I lay
Vanquished and faint, the grasp of bloody hands
I felt, and saw on high the glare of falling brands,

19.
When on my foes a sudden terror came,
And they fled, scattering lo! with reinless speed
A black Tartarian horse of giant frame
Comes trampling over the dead, the living bleed
Beneath the hoofs of that tremendous steed,
On which, like to an Angel, robed in white,
Sate one waving a sword; the hosts recede
And fly, as through their ranks with awful might,
Sweeps in the shadow of eve that Phantom swift and bright;

20.
And its path made a solitude. I rose
And marked its coming: it relaxed its course
As it approached me, and the wind that flows
Through night, bore accents to mine ear whose force
Might create smiles in death, the Tartar horse
Paused, and I saw the shape its might which swayed,
And heard her musical pants, like the sweet source
Of waters in the desert, as she said,
'Mount with me, Laon, now' I rapidly obeyed.

21.
Then: 'Away! away!' she cried, and stretched her sword
As 'twere a scourge over the courser's head,
And lightly shook the reins. We spake no word,
But like the vapour of the tempest fled
Over the plain; her dark hair was dispread
Like the pine's locks upon the lingering blast;
Over mine eyes its shadowy strings it spread
Fitfully, and the hills and streams fled fast,
As o'er their glimmering forms the steed's broad shadow passed.

22.
And his hoofs ground the rocks to fire and dust,
His strong sides made the torrents rise in spray,
And turbulence, as of a whirlwind's gust
Surrounded us; and still away! away!
Through the desert night we sped, while she alway
Gazed on a mountain which we neared, whose crest,
Crowned with a marble ruin, in the ray
Of the obscure stars gleamed; its rugged breast

The steed strained up, and then his impulse did arrest.

23.
A rocky hill which overhung the Ocean:
From that lone ruin, when the steed that panted
Paused, might be heard the murmur of the motion
Of waters, as in spots for ever haunted
By the choicest winds of Heaven, which are enchanted
To music, by the wand of Solitude,
That wizard wild, and the far tents implanted
Upon the plain, be seen by those who stood
Thence marking the dark shore of Ocean's curved flood.

24.
One moment these were heard and seen another
Passed; and the two who stood beneath that night,
Each only heard, or saw, or felt the other;
As from the lofty steed she did alight,
Cythna, (for, from the eyes whose deepest light
Of love and sadness made my lips feel pale
With influence strange of mournfullest delight,
My own sweet Cythna looked), with joy did quail,
And felt her strength in tears of human weakness fail.

25.
And for a space in my embrace she rested,
Her head on my unquiet heart reposing,
While my faint arms her languid frame invested;
At length she looked on me, and half unclosing
Her tremulous lips, said, 'Friend, thy bands were losing
The battle, as I stood before the King
In bonds. I burst them then, and swiftly choosing
The time, did seize a Tartar's sword, and spring
Upon his horse, and swift, as on the whirlwind's wing,

26.
'Have thou and I been borne beyond pursuer,
And we are here.' Then, turning to the steed,
She pressed the white moon on his front with pure
And rose-like lips, and many a fragrant weed
From the green ruin plucked, that he might feed;
But I to a stone seat that Maiden led,
And, kissing her fair eyes, said, 'Thou hast need
Of rest,' and I heaped up the courser's bed
In a green mossy nook, with mountain flowers dispread.

27.

Within that ruin, where a shattered portal
Looks to the eastern stars, abandoned now
By man, to be the home of things immortal,
Memories, like awful ghosts which come and go,
And must inherit all he builds below,
When he is gone, a hall stood; o'er whose roof
Fair clinging weeds with ivy pale did grow,
Clasping its gray rents with a verdurous woof,
A hanging dome of leaves, a canopy moon-proof.

28.
The autumnal winds, as if spell-bound, had made
A natural couch of leaves in that recess,
Which seasons none disturbed, but, in the shade
Of flowering parasites, did Spring love to dress
With their sweet blooms the wintry loneliness
Of those dead leaves, shedding their stars, whene'er
The wandering wind her nurslings might caress;
Whose intertwining fingers ever there
Made music wild and soft that filled the listening air.

29.
We know not where we go, or what sweet dream
May pilot us through caverns strange and fair
Of far and pathless passion, while the stream
Of life, our bark doth on its whirlpools bear,
Spreading swift wings as sails to the dim air;
Nor should we seek to know, so the devotion
Of love and gentle thoughts be heard still there
Louder and louder from the utmost Ocean
Of universal life, attuning its commotion.

30.
To the pure all things are pure! Oblivion wrapped
Our spirits, and the fearful overthrow
Of public hope was from our being snapped,
Though linked years had bound it there; for now
A power, a thirst, a knowledge, which below
All thoughts, like light beyond the atmosphere,
Clothing its clouds with grace, doth ever flow,
Came on us, as we sate in silence there,
Beneath the golden stars of the clear azure air;

31.
In silence which doth follow talk that causes
The baffled heart to speak with sighs and tears,
When wildering passion swalloweth up the pauses

Of inexpressive speech: the youthful years
Which we together passed, their hopes and fears,
The blood itself which ran within our frames,
That likeness of the features which endears
The thoughts expressed by them, our very names,
And all the winged hours which speechless memory claims,

32.
Had found a voice and ere that voice did pass,
The night grew damp and dim, and, through a rent
Of the ruin where we sate, from the morass
A wandering Meteor by some wild wind sent,
Hung high in the green dome, to which it lent
A faint and pallid lustre; while the song
Of blasts, in which its blue hair quivering bent,
Strewed strangest sounds the moving leaves among;
A wondrous light, the sound as of a spirit's tongue.

33.
The Meteor showed the leaves on which we sate,
And Cythna's glowing arms, and the thick ties
Of her soft hair, which bent with gathered weight
My neck near hers; her dark and deepening eyes,
Which, as twin phantoms of one star that lies
O'er a dim well, move, though the star reposes,
Swam in our mute and liquid ecstasies,
Her marble brow, and eager lips, like roses,
With their own fragrance pale, which Spring but half uncloses.

34.
The Meteor to its far morass returned:
The beating of our veins one interval
Made still; and then I felt the blood that burned
Within her frame, mingle with mine, and fall
Around my heart like fire; and over all
A mist was spread, the sickness of a deep
And speechless swoon of joy, as might befall
Two disunited spirits when they leap
In union from this earth's obscure and fading sleep.

35.
Was it one moment that confounded thus
All thought, all sense, all feeling, into one
Unutterable power, which shielded us
Even from our own cold looks, when we had gone
Into a wide and wild oblivion
Of tumult and of tenderness? or now

Had ages, such as make the moon and sun,
The seasons, and mankind their changes know,
Left fear and time unfelt by us alone below?

36.
I know not. What are kisses whose fire clasps
The failing heart in languishment, or limb
Twined within limb? or the quick dying gasps
Of the life meeting, when the faint eyes swim
Through tears of a wide mist boundless and dim,
In one caress? What is the strong control
Which leads the heart that dizzy steep to climb,
Where far over the world those vapours roll
Which blend two restless frames in one reposing soul?
37.
It is the shadow which doth float unseen,
But not unfelt, o'er blind mortality,
Whose divine darkness fled not from that green
And lone recess, where lapped in peace did lie
Our linked frames, till, from the changing sky
That night and still another day had fled;
And then I saw and felt. The moon was high,
And clouds, as of a coming storm, were spread
Under its orb, loud winds were gathering overhead.

38.
Cythna's sweet lips seemed lurid in the moon,
Her fairest limbs with the night wind were chill,
And her dark tresses were all loosely strewn
O'er her pale bosom: all within was still,
And the sweet peace of joy did almost fill
The depth of her unfathomable look;
And we sate calmly, though that rocky hill,
The waves contending in its caverns strook,
For they foreknew the storm, and the gray ruin shook.

39.
There we unheeding sate, in the communion
Of interchanged vows, which, with a rite
Of faith most sweet and sacred, stamped our union.
Few were the living hearts which could unite
Like ours, or celebrate a bridal night
With such close sympathies, for they had sprung
From linked youth, and from the gentle might
Of earliest love, delayed and cherished long,
Which common hopes and fears made, like a tempest, strong.

40.
And such is Nature's law divine, that those
Who grow together cannot choose but love,
If faith or custom do not interpose,
Or common slavery mar what else might move
All gentlest thoughts; as in the sacred grove
Which shades the springs of Ethiopian Nile,
That living tree which, if the arrowy dove
Strike with her shadow, shrinks in fear awhile,
But its own kindred leaves clasps while the sunbeams smile;

41.
And clings to them, when darkness may dissever
The close caresses of all duller plants
Which bloom on the wide earth, thus we for ever
Were linked, for love had nursed us in the haunts
Where knowledge, from its secret source enchants
Young hearts with the fresh music of its springing,
Ere yet its gathered flood feeds human wants,
As the great Nile feeds Egypt; ever flinging
Light on the woven boughs which o'er its waves are swinging.

42.
The tones of Cythna's voice like echoes were
Of those far murmuring streams; they rose and fell,
Mixed with mine own in the tempestuous air,
And so we sate, until our talk befell
Of the late ruin, swift and horrible,
And how those seeds of hope might yet be sown,
Whose fruit is evil's mortal poison: well,
For us, this ruin made a watch-tower lone,
But Cythna's eyes looked faint, and now two days were gone

43.
Since she had food: therefore I did awaken
The Tartar steed, who, from his ebon mane
Soon as the clinging slumbers he had shaken,
Bent his thin head to seek the brazen rein,
Following me obediently; with pain
Of heart, so deep and dread, that one caress,
When lips and heart refuse to part again
Till they have told their fill, could scarce express
The anguish of her mute and fearful tenderness,

44.
Cythna beheld me part, as I bestrode
That willing steed the tempest and the night,

Which gave my path its safety as I rode
Down the ravine of rocks, did soon unite
The darkness and the tumult of their might
Borne on all winds. Far through the streaming rain
Floating at intervals the garments white
Of Cythna gleamed, and her voice once again
Came to me on the gust, and soon I reached the plain.

45.
I dreaded not the tempest, nor did he
Who bore me, but his eyeballs wide and red
Turned on the lightning's cleft exultingly;
And when the earth beneath his tameless tread,
Shook with the sullen thunder, he would spread
His nostrils to the blast, and joyously
Mock the fierce peal with neighings; thus we sped
O'er the lit plain, and soon I could descry
Where Death and Fire had gorged the spoil of victory.

46.
There was a desolate village in a wood
Whose bloom-inwoven leaves now scattering fed
The hungry storm; it was a place of blood,
A heap of hearthless walls; the flames were dead
Within those dwellings now, the life had fled
From all those corpses now, but the wide sky
Flooded with lightning was ribbed overhead
By the black rafters, and around did lie
Women, and babes, and men, slaughtered confusedly.

47.
Beside the fountain in the market-place
Dismounting, I beheld those corpses stare
With horny eyes upon each other's face,
And on the earth and on the vacant air,
And upon me, close to the waters where
I stooped to slake my thirst; I shrank to taste,
For the salt bitterness of blood was there;
But tied the steed beside, and sought in haste
If any yet survived amid that ghastly waste.

48.
No living thing was there beside one woman,
Whom I found wandering in the streets, and she
Was withered from a likeness of aught human
Into a fiend, by some strange misery:
Soon as she heard my steps she leaped on me,

And glued her burning lips to mine, and laughed
With a loud, long, and frantic laugh of glee,
And cried, 'Now, Mortal, thou hast deeply quaffed
The Plague's blue kisses soon millions shall pledge the draught!

49.
'My name is Pestilence, this bosom dry,
Once fed two babes, a sister and a brother
When I came home, one in the blood did lie
Of three death-wounds, the flames had ate the other!
Since then I have no longer been a mother,
But I am Pestilence; hither and thither
I flit about, that I may slay and smother:
All lips which I have kissed must surely wither,
But Death's, if thou art he, we'll go to work together!

50.
'What seek'st thou here? The moonlight comes in flashes,
The dew is rising dankly from the dell
'Twill moisten her! and thou shalt see the gashes
In my sweet boy, now full of worms but tell
First what thou seek'st.' - 'I seek for food.' - ''Tis well,
Thou shalt have food. Famine, my paramour,
Waits for us at the feast, cruel and fell
Is Famine, but he drives not from his door
Those whom these lips have kissed, alone. No more, no more!'

51.
As thus she spake, she grasped me with the strength
Of madness, and by many a ruined hearth
She led, and over many a corpse: at length
We came to a lone hut where on the earth
Which made its floor, she in her ghastly mirth,
Gathering from all those homes now desolate,
Had piled three heaps of loaves, making a dearth
Among the dead, round which she set in state
A ring of cold, stiff babes; silent and stark they sate.

52.
She leaped upon a pile, and lifted high
Her mad looks to the lightning, and cried: 'Eat!
Share the great feast, to-morrow we must die!'
And then she spurned the loaves with her pale feet,
Towards her bloodless guests; that sight to meet,
Mine eyes and my heart ached, and but that she
Who loved me, did with absent looks defeat
Despair, I might have raved in sympathy;

But now I took the food that woman offered me;

53.
And vainly having with her madness striven
If I might win her to return with me,
Departed. In the eastern beams of Heaven
The lightning now grew pallid, rapidly,
As by the shore of the tempestuous sea
The dark steed bore me; and the mountain gray
Soon echoed to his hoofs, and I could see
Cythna among the rocks, where she alway
Had sate with anxious eyes fixed on the lingering day.

54.
And joy was ours to meet: she was most pale,
Famished, and wet and weary, so I cast
My arms around her, lest her steps should fail
As to our home we went, and thus embraced,
Her full heart seemed a deeper joy to taste
Than e'er the prosperous know; the steed behind
Trod peacefully along the mountain waste;
We reached our home ere morning could unbind
Night's latest veil, and on our bridal-couch reclined.

55.
Her chilled heart having cherished in my bosom,
And sweetest kisses past, we two did share
Our peaceful meal: as an autumnal blossom
Which spreads its shrunk leaves in the sunny air,
After cold showers, like rainbows woven there,
Thus in her lips and cheeks the vital spirit
Mantled, and in her eyes, an atmosphere
Of health, and hope; and sorrow languished near it,
And fear, and all that dark despondence doth inherit.

CANTO 7.

1.
So we sate joyous as the morning ray
Which fed upon the wrecks of night and storm
Now lingering on the winds; light airs did play
Among the dewy weeds, the sun was warm,
And we sate linked in the inwoven charm
Of converse and caresses sweet and deep,
Speechless caresses, talk that might disarm

Time, though he wield the darts of death and sleep,
And those thrice mortal barbs in his own poison steep.

2.
I told her of my sufferings and my madness,
And how, awakened from that dreamy mood
By Liberty's uprise, the strength of gladness
Came to my spirit in my solitude;
And all that now I was, while tears pursued
Each other down her fair and listening cheek
Fast as the thoughts which fed them, like a flood
From sunbright dales; and when I ceased to speak,
Her accents soft and sweet the pausing air did wake.

3.
She told me a strange tale of strange endurance,
Like broken memories of many a heart
Woven into one; to which no firm assurance,
So wild were they, could her own faith impart.
She said that not a tear did dare to start
From the swoln brain, and that her thoughts were firm
When from all mortal hope she did depart,
Borne by those slaves across the Ocean's term,
And that she reached the port without one fear infirm.

4.
One was she among many there, the thralls
Of the cold Tyrant's cruel lust; and they
Laughed mournfully in those polluted halls;
But she was calm and sad, musing alway
On loftiest enterprise, till on a day
The Tyrant heard her singing to her lute
A wild, and sad, and spirit-thrilling lay,
Like winds that die in wastes, one moment mute
The evil thoughts it made, which did his breast pollute.

5.
Even when he saw her wondrous loveliness,
One moment to great Nature's sacred power
He bent, and was no longer passionless;
But when he bade her to his secret bower
Be borne, a loveless victim, and she tore
Her locks in agony, and her words of flame
And mightier looks availed not; then he bore
Again his load of slavery, and became
A king, a heartless beast, a pageant and a name.

6.
She told me what a loathsome agony
Is that when selfishness mocks love's delight,
Foul as in dream's most fearful imagery,
To dally with the mowing dead, that night
All torture, fear, or horror made seem light
Which the soul dreams or knows, and when the day
Shone on her awful frenzy, from the sight
Where like a Spirit in fleshly chains she lay
Struggling, aghast and pale the Tyrant fled away.

7.
Her madness was a beam of light, a power
Which dawned through the rent soul; and words it gave,
Gestures and looks, such as in whirlwinds bore
Which might not be withstood, whence none could save
All who approached their sphere, like some calm wave
Vexed into whirlpools by the chasms beneath;
And sympathy made each attendant slave
Fearless and free, and they began to breathe
Deep curses, like the voice of flames far underneath.

8.
The King felt pale upon his noonday throne:
At night two slaves he to her chamber sent,
One was a green and wrinkled eunuch, grown
From human shape into an instrument
Of all things ill, distorted, bowed and bent.
The other was a wretch from infancy
Made dumb by poison; who nought knew or meant
But to obey: from the fire isles came he,
A diver lean and strong, of Oman's coral sea.

9.
They bore her to a bark, and the swift stroke
Of silent rowers clove the blue moonlight seas,
Until upon their path the morning broke;
They anchored then, where, be there calm or breeze,
The gloomiest of the drear Symplegades
Shakes with the sleepless surge; the Ethiop there
Wound his long arms around her, and with knees
Like iron clasped her feet, and plunged with her
Among the closing waves out of the boundless air.

10.
'Swift as an eagle stooping from the plain
Of morning light, into some shadowy wood,

He plunged through the green silence of the main,
Through many a cavern which the eternal flood
Had scooped, as dark lairs for its monster brood;
And among mighty shapes which fled in wonder,
And among mightier shadows which pursued
His heels, he wound: until the dark rocks under
He touched a golden chain, a sound arose like thunder.

11.
'A stunning clang of massive bolts redoubling
Beneath the deep, a burst of waters driven
As from the roots of the sea, raging and bubbling:
And in that roof of crags a space was riven
Through which there shone the emerald beams of heaven,
Shot through the lines of many waves inwoven,
Like sunlight through acacia woods at even,
Through which, his way the diver having cloven,
Passed like a spark sent up out of a burning oven.

12.
'And then,' she said, 'he laid me in a cave
Above the waters, by that chasm of sea,
A fountain round and vast, in which the wave
Imprisoned, boiled and leaped perpetually,
Down which, one moment resting, he did flee,
Winning the adverse depth; that spacious cell
Like an hupaithric temple wide and high,
Whose aery dome is inaccessible,
Was pierced with one round cleft through which the sunbeams fell.

13.
'Below, the fountain's brink was richly paven
With the deep's wealth, coral, and pearl, and sand
Like spangling gold, and purple shells engraven
With mystic legends by no mortal hand,
Left there, when thronging to the moon's command,
The gathering waves rent the Hesperian gate
Of mountains, and on such bright floor did stand
Columns, and shapes like statues, and the state
Of kingless thrones, which Earth did in her heart create.

14.
'The fiend of madness which had made its prey
Of my poor heart, was lulled to sleep awhile:
There was an interval of many a day,
And a sea-eagle brought me food the while,
Whose nest was built in that untrodden isle,

And who, to be the gaoler had been taught
Of that strange dungeon; as a friend whose smile
Like light and rest at morn and even is sought
That wild bird was to me, till madness misery brought.

15.
'The misery of a madness slow and creeping,
Which made the earth seem fire, the sea seem air,
And the white clouds of noon which oft were sleeping,
In the blue heaven so beautiful and fair,
Like hosts of ghastly shadows hovering there;
And the sea-eagle looked a fiend, who bore
Thy mangled limbs for food! Thus all things were
Transformed into the agony which I wore
Even as a poisoned robe around my bosom's core.

16.
'Again I knew the day and night fast fleeing,
The eagle, and the fountain, and the air;
Another frenzy came, there seemed a being
Within me, a strange load my heart did bear,
As if some living thing had made its lair
Even in the fountains of my life: a long
And wondrous vision wrought from my despair,
Then grew, like sweet reality among
Dim visionary woes, an unreposing throng.

17.
'Methought I was about to be a mother
Month after month went by, and still I dreamed
That we should soon be all to one another,
I and my child; and still new pulses seemed
To beat beside my heart, and still I deemed
There was a babe within and, when the rain
Of winter through the rifted cavern streamed,
Methought, after a lapse of lingering pain,
I saw that lovely shape, which near my heart had lain.

18.
'It was a babe, beautiful from its birth,
It was like thee, dear love, its eyes were thine,
Its brow, its lips, and so upon the earth
It laid its fingers, as now rest on mine
Thine own, beloved! 'twas a dream divine;
Even to remember how it fled, how swift,
How utterly, might make the heart repine,
Though 'twas a dream.' Then Cythna did uplift

Her looks on mine, as if some doubt she sought to shift:

19.
A doubt which would not flee, a tenderness
Of questioning grief, a source of thronging tears;
Which having passed, as one whom sobs oppress
She spoke: 'Yes, in the wilderness of years
Her memory, aye, like a green home appears;
She sucked her fill even at this breast, sweet love,
For many months. I had no mortal fears;
Methought I felt her lips and breath approve,
It was a human thing which to my bosom clove.

20.
'I watched the dawn of her first smiles; and soon
When zenith stars were trembling on the wave,
Or when the beams of the invisible moon,
Or sun, from many a prism within the cave
Their gem-born shadows to the water gave,
Her looks would hunt them, and with outspread hand,
From the swift lights which might that fountain pave,
She would mark one, and laugh, when that command
Slighting, it lingered there, and could not understand.

21.
'Methought her looks began to talk with me;
And no articulate sounds, but something sweet
Her lips would frame, so sweet it could not be,
That it was meaningless; her touch would meet
Mine, and our pulses calmly flow and beat
In response while we slept; and on a day
When I was happiest in that strange retreat,
With heaps of golden shells we two did play,
Both infants, weaving wings for time's perpetual way.

22.
'Ere night, methought, her waning eyes were grown
Weary with joy, and tired with our delight,
We, on the earth, like sister twins lay down
On one fair mother's bosom: from that night
She fled, like those illusions clear and bright,
Which dwell in lakes, when the red moon on high
Pause ere it wakens tempest; and her flight,
Though 'twas the death of brainless fantasy,
Yet smote my lonesome heart more than all misery.

23.

'It seemed that in the dreary night the diver
Who brought me thither, came again, and bore
My child away. I saw the waters quiver,
When he so swiftly sunk, as once before:
Then morning came, it shone even as of yore,
But I was changed, the very life was gone
Out of my heart, I wasted more and more,
Day after day, and sitting there alone,
Vexed the inconstant waves with my perpetual moan.

24.
'I was no longer mad, and yet methought
My breasts were swoln and changed: in every vein
The blood stood still one moment, while that thought
Was passing with a gush of sickening pain
It ebbed even to its withered springs again:
When my wan eyes in stern resolve I turned
From that most strange delusion, which would fain
Have waked the dream for which my spirit yearned
With more than human love, then left it unreturned.

25.
'So now my reason was restored to me
I struggled with that dream, which, like a beast
Most fierce and beauteous, in my memory
Had made its lair, and on my heart did feast;
But all that cave and all its shapes, possessed
By thoughts which could not fade, renewed each one
Some smile, some look, some gesture which had blessed
Me heretofore: I, sitting there alone,
Vexed the inconstant waves with my perpetual moan.

26.
'Time passed, I know not whether months or years;
For day, nor night, nor change of seasons made
Its note, but thoughts and unavailing tears:
And I became at last even as a shade,
A smoke, a cloud on which the winds have preyed,
Till it be thin as air; until, one even,
A Nautilus upon the fountain played,
Spreading his azure sail where breath of Heaven
Descended not, among the waves and whirlpools driven.

27.
'And, when the Eagle came, that lovely thing,
Oaring with rosy feet its silver boat,
Fled near me as for shelter; on slow wing,

The Eagle, hovering o'er his prey did float;
But when he saw that I with fear did note
His purpose, proffering my own food to him,
The eager plumes subsided on his throat
He came where that bright child of sea did swim,
And o'er it cast in peace his shadow broad and dim.

28.
'This wakened me, it gave me human strength;
And hope, I know not whence or wherefore, rose,
But I resumed my ancient powers at length;
My spirit felt again like one of those
Like thine, whose fate it is to make the woes
Of humankind their prey, what was this cave?
Its deep foundation no firm purpose knows
Immutable, resistless, strong to save,
Like mind while yet it mocks the all-devouring grave.

29.
'And where was Laon? might my heart be dead,
While that far dearer heart could move and be?
Or whilst over the earth the pall was spread,
Which I had sworn to rend? I might be free,
Could I but win that friendly bird to me,
To bring me ropes; and long in vain I sought
By intercourse of mutual imagery
Of objects, if such aid he could be taught;
But fruit, and flowers, and boughs, yet never ropes he brought.

30.
'We live in our own world, and mine was made
From glorious fantasies of hope departed:
Aye we are darkened with their floating shade,
Or cast a lustre on them, time imparted
Such power to me, I became fearless-hearted,
My eye and voice grew firm, calm was my mind,
And piercing, like the morn, now it has darted
Its lustre on all hidden things, behind
Yon dim and fading clouds which load the weary wind.

31.
'My mind became the book through which I grew
Wise in all human wisdom, and its cave,
Which like a mine I rifled through and through,
To me the keeping of its secrets gave
One mind, the type of all, the moveless wave
Whose calm reflects all moving things that are,

Necessity, and love, and life, the grave,
And sympathy, fountains of hope and fear,
Justice, and truth, and time, and the world's natural sphere.

32.
'And on the sand would I make signs to range
These woofs, as they were woven, of my thought;
Clear, elemental shapes, whose smallest change
A subtler language within language wrought:
The key of truths which once were dimly taught
In old Crotona; and sweet melodies
Of love, in that lorn solitude I caught
From mine own voice in dream, when thy dear eyes
Shone through my sleep, and did that utterance harmonize.

33.
'Thy songs were winds whereon I fled at will,
As in a winged chariot, o'er the plain
Of crystal youth; and thou wert there to fill
My heart with joy, and there we sate again
On the gray margin of the glimmering main,
Happy as then but wiser far, for we
Smiled on the flowery grave in which were lain
Fear, Faith and Slavery; and mankind was free,
Equal, and pure, and wise, in Wisdom's prophecy.

34.
'For to my will my fancies were as slaves
To do their sweet and subtile ministries;
And oft from that bright fountain's shadowy waves
They would make human throngs gather and rise
To combat with my overflowing eyes,
And voice made deep with passion, thus I grew
Familiar with the shock and the surprise
And war of earthly minds, from which I drew
The power which has been mine to frame their thoughts anew.

35.
'And thus my prison was the populous earth
Where I saw even as misery dreams of morn
Before the east has given its glory birth
Religion's pomp made desolate by the scorn
Of Wisdom's faintest smile, and thrones uptorn,
And dwellings of mild people interspersed
With undivided fields of ripening corn,
And love made free, a hope which we have nursed
Even with our blood and tears, until its glory burst.

36.
'All is not lost! There is some recompense
For hope whose fountain can be thus profound,
Even throned Evil's splendid impotence,
Girt by its hell of power, the secret sound
Of hymns to truth and freedom the dread bound
Of life and death passed fearlessly and well,
Dungeons wherein the high resolve is found,
Racks which degraded woman's greatness tell,
And what may else be good and irresistible.

37.
'Such are the thoughts which, like the fires that flare
In storm-encompassed isles, we cherish yet
In this dark ruin such were mine even there;
As in its sleep some odorous violet,
While yet its leaves with nightly dews are wet,
Breathes in prophetic dreams of day's uprise,
Or as, ere Scythian frost in fear has met
Spring's messengers descending from the skies,
The buds foreknow their life this hope must ever rise.

38.
'So years had passed, when sudden earthquake rent
The depth of ocean, and the cavern cracked
With sound, as if the world's wide continent
Had fallen in universal ruin wracked:
And through the cleft streamed in one cataract
The stifling waters, when I woke, the flood
Whose banded waves that crystal cave had sacked
Was ebbing round me, and my bright abode
Before me yawned, a chasm desert, and bare, and broad.

39.
'Above me was the sky, beneath the sea:
I stood upon a point of shattered stone,
And heard loose rocks rushing tumultuously
With splash and shock into the deep, anon
All ceased, and there was silence wide and lone.
I felt that I was free! The Ocean-spray
Quivered beneath my feet, the broad Heaven shone
Around, and in my hair the winds did play
Lingering as they pursued their unimpeded way.

40.
'My spirit moved upon the sea like wind

Which round some thymy cape will lag and hover,
Though it can wake the still cloud, and unbind
The strength of tempest: day was almost over,
When through the fading light I could discover
A ship approaching, its white sails were fed
With the north wind, its moving shade did cover
The twilight deep; the mariners in dread
Cast anchor when they saw new rocks around them spread.

41.
'And when they saw one sitting on a crag,
They sent a boat to me; the Sailors rowed
In awe through many a new and fearful jag
Of overhanging rock, through which there flowed
The foam of streams that cannot make abode.
They came and questioned me, but when they heard
My voice, they became silent, and they stood
And moved as men in whom new love had stirred
Deep thoughts: so to the ship we passed without a word.

CANTO 8.

1.
'I sate beside the Steersman then, and gazing
Upon the west, cried, "Spread the sails! Behold!
The sinking moon is like a watch-tower blazing
Over the mountains yet; the City of Gold
Yon Cape alone does from the sight withhold;
The stream is fleet, the north breathes steadily
Beneath the stars; they tremble with the cold!
Ye cannot rest upon the dreary sea!
Haste, haste to the warm home of happier destiny!"

2.
'The Mariners obeyed, the Captain stood
Aloof, and, whispering to the Pilot, said,
"Alas, alas! I fear we are pursued
By wicked ghosts; a Phantom of the Dead,
The night before we sailed, came to my bed
In dream, like that!" The Pilot then replied,
"It cannot be, she is a human Maid
Her low voice makes you weep, she is some bride,
Or daughter of high birth, she can be nought beside."

3.

'We passed the islets, borne by wind and stream,
And as we sailed, the Mariners came near
And thronged around to listen; in the gleam
Of the pale moon I stood, as one whom fear
May not attaint, and my calm voice did rear;
"Ye are all human, yon broad moon gives light
To millions who the selfsame likeness wear,
Even while I speak beneath this very night,
Their thoughts flow on like ours, in sadness or delight.

4.
'"What dream ye? Your own hands have built an home,
Even for yourselves on a beloved shore:
For some, fond eyes are pining till they come,
How they will greet him when his toils are o'er,
And laughing babes rush from the well-known door!
Is this your care? ye toil for your own good
Ye feel and think, has some immortal power
Such purposes? or in a human mood,
Dream ye some Power thus builds for man in solitude?

5.
'"What is that Power? Ye mock yourselves, and give
A human heart to what ye cannot know:
As if the cause of life could think and live!
'Twere as if man's own works should feel, and show
The hopes, and fears, and thoughts from which they flow,
And he be like to them! Lo! Plague is free
To waste, Blight, Poison, Earthquake, Hail, and Snow,
Disease, and Want, and worse Necessity
Of hate and ill, and Pride, and Fear, and Tyranny!

6.
'"What is that Power? Some moon-struck sophist stood
Watching the shade from his own soul upthrown
Fill Heaven and darken Earth, and in such mood
The Form he saw and worshipped was his own,
His likeness in the world's vast mirror shown;
And 'twere an innocent dream, but that a faith
Nursed by fear's dew of poison, grows thereon,
And that men say, that Power has chosen Death
On all who scorn its laws, to wreak immortal wrath.

7.
'"Men say that they themselves have heard and seen,
Or known from others who have known such things,
A Shade, a Form, which Earth and Heaven between

Wields an invisible rod, that Priests and Kings,
Custom, domestic sway, ay, all that brings
Man's freeborn soul beneath the oppressor's heel,
Are his strong ministers, and that the stings
Of death will make the wise his vengeance feel,
Though truth and virtue arm their hearts with tenfold steel.

8.
"'And it is said, this Power will punish wrong;
Yes, add despair to crime, and pain to pain!
And deepest hell, and deathless snakes among,
Will bind the wretch on whom is fixed a stain,
Which, like a plague, a burden, and a bane,
Clung to him while he lived; for love and hate,
Virtue and vice, they say are difference vain
The will of strength is right, this human state
Tyrants, that they may rule, with lies thus desolate.

9.
"'Alas, what strength? Opinion is more frail
Than yon dim cloud now fading on the moon
Even while we gaze, though it awhile avail
To hide the orb of truth and every throne
Of Earth or Heaven, though shadow, rests thereon,
One shape of many names: for this ye plough
The barren waves of ocean, hence each one
Is slave or tyrant; all betray and bow,
Command, or kill, or fear, or wreak, or suffer woe.

10.
"'Its names are each a sign which maketh holy
All power, ay, the ghost, the dream, the shade
Of power, lust, falsehood, hate, and pride, and folly;
The pattern whence all fraud and wrong is made,
A law to which mankind has been betrayed;
And human love, is as the name well known
Of a dear mother, whom the murderer laid
In bloody grave, and into darkness thrown,
Gathered her wildered babes around him as his own.

11.
"'O Love, who to the hearts of wandering men
Art as the calm to Ocean's weary waves!
Justice, or Truth, or Joy! those only can
From slavery and religion's labyrinth caves
Guide us, as one clear star the seaman saves.
To give to all an equal share of good,

To track the steps of Freedom, though through graves
She pass, to suffer all in patient mood,
To weep for crime, though stained with thy friend's dearest blood,

12.
"'To feel the peace of self-contentment's lot,
To own all sympathies, and outrage none,
And in the inmost bowers of sense and thought,
Until life's sunny day is quite gone down,
To sit and smile with Joy, or, not alone,
To kiss salt tears from the worn cheek of Woe;
To live, as if to love and live were one,
This is not faith or law, nor those who bow
To thrones on Heaven or Earth, such destiny may know.

13.
"'But children near their parents tremble now,
Because they must obey, one rules another,
And as one Power rules both high and low,
So man is made the captive of his brother,
And Hate is throned on high with Fear her mother,
Above the Highest and those fountain-cells,
Whence love yet flowed when faith had choked all other,
Are darkened. Woman as the bond-slave dwells
Of man, a slave; and life is poisoned in its wells.

14.
"'Man seeks for gold in mines, that he may weave
A lasting chain for his own slavery;
In fear and restless care that he may live
He toils for others, who must ever be
The joyless thralls of like captivity;
He murders, for his chiefs delight in ruin;
He builds the altar, that its idol's fee
May be his very blood; he is pursuing
O, blind and willing wretch! his own obscure undoing.

15.
"'Woman! she is his slave, she has become
A thing I weep to speak the child of scorn,
The outcast of a desolated home;
Falsehood, and fear, and toil, like waves have worn
Channels upon her cheek, which smiles adorn,
As calm decks the false Ocean: well ye know
What Woman is, for none of Woman born
Can choose but drain the bitter dregs of woe,
Whichever from the oppressed to the oppressors flow.

16.
"'This need not be; ye might arise, and will
That gold should lose its power, and thrones their glory;
That love, which none may bind, be free to fill
The world, like light; and evil faith, grown hoary
With crime, be quenched and die. Yon promontory
Even now eclipses the descending moon!
Dungeons and palaces are transitory
High temples fade like vapour. Man alone
Remains, whose will has power when all beside is gone.

17.
"'Let all be free and equal! From your hearts
I feel an echo; through my inmost frame
Like sweetest sound, seeking its mate, it darts
Whence come ye, friends? Alas, I cannot name
All that I read of sorrow, toil, and shame,
On your worn faces; as in legends old
Which make immortal the disastrous fame
Of conquerors and impostors false and bold,
The discord of your hearts, I in your looks behold.

18.
"'Whence come ye, friends? from pouring human blood
Forth on the earth? Or bring ye steel and gold,
That Kings may dupe and slay the multitude?
Or from the famished poor, pale, weak and cold,
Bear ye the earnings of their toil? Unfold!
Speak! Are your hands in slaughter's sanguine hue
Stained freshly? have your hearts in guile grown old?
Know yourselves thus! ye shall be pure as dew,
And I will be a friend and sister unto you.

19.
"'Disguise it not, we have one human heart
All mortal thoughts confess a common home:
Blush not for what may to thyself impart
Stains of inevitable crime: the doom
Is this, which has, or may, or must become
Thine, and all humankind's. Ye are the spoil
Which Time thus marks for the devouring tomb
Thou and thy thoughts and they, and all the toil
Wherewith ye twine the rings of life's perpetual coil.

20.
"'Disguise it not, ye blush for what ye hate,

And Enmity is sister unto Shame;
Look on your mind, it is the book of fate
Ah! it is dark with many a blazoned name
Of misery, all are mirrors of the same;
But the dark fiend who with his iron pen
Dipped in scorn's fiery poison, makes his fame
Enduring there, would o'er the heads of men
Pass harmless, if they scorned to make their hearts his den.

21.
"'Yes, it is Hate, that shapeless fiendly thing
Of many names, all evil, some divine,
Whom self-contempt arms with a mortal sting;
Which, when the heart its snaky folds entwine
Is wasted quite, and when it doth repine
To gorge such bitter prey, on all beside
It turns with ninefold rage, as with its twine
When Amphisbaena some fair bird has tied,
Soon o'er the putrid mass he threats on every side.

22.
"'Reproach not thine own soul, but know thyself,
Nor hate another's crime, nor loathe thine own.
It is the dark idolatry of self,
Which, when our thoughts and actions once are gone,
Demands that man should weep, and bleed, and groan;
Oh, vacant expiation! Be at rest.
The past is Death's, the future is thine own;
And love and joy can make the foulest breast
A paradise of flowers, where peace might build her nest.

23.
"'Speak thou! whence come ye?" A Youth made reply:
"Wearily, wearily o'er the boundless deep
We sail; thou readest well the misery
Told in these faded eyes, but much doth sleep
Within, which there the poor heart loves to keep,
Or dare not write on the dishonoured brow;
Even from our childhood have we learned to steep
The bread of slavery in the tears of woe,
And never dreamed of hope or refuge until now.

24.
"'Yes, I must speak, my secret should have perished
Even with the heart it wasted, as a brand
Fades in the dying flame whose life it cherished,
But that no human bosom can withstand

Thee, wondrous Lady, and the mild command
Of thy keen eyes: yes, we are wretched slaves,
Who from their wonted loves and native land
Are reft, and bear o'er the dividing waves
The unregarded prey of calm and happy graves.

25.
'"We drag afar from pastoral vales the fairest
Among the daughters of those mountains lone,
We drag them there, where all things best and rarest
Are stained and trampled: years have come and gone
Since, like the ship which bears me, I have known
No thought; but now the eyes of one dear Maid
On mine with light of mutual love have shone
She is my life, I am but as the shade
Of her, a smoke sent up from ashes, soon to fade.

26.
'"For she must perish in the Tyrant's hall
Alas, alas!" He ceased, and by the sail
Sate cowering but his sobs were heard by all,
And still before the ocean and the gale
The ship fled fast till the stars 'gan to fail;
And, round me gathered with mute countenance,
The Seamen gazed, the Pilot, worn and pale
With toil, the Captain with gray locks, whose glance
Met mine in restless awe, they stood as in a trance.

27.
'"Recede not! pause not now! Thou art grown old,
But Hope will make thee young, for Hope and Youth
Are children of one mother, even Love behold!
The eternal stars gaze on us! is the truth
Within your soul? care for your own, or ruth
For others' sufferings? do ye thirst to bear
A heart which not the serpent Custom's tooth
May violate? Be free! and even here,
Swear to be firm till death!" They cried, "We swear! We swear!"

28.
'The very darkness shook, as with a blast
Of subterranean thunder, at the cry;
The hollow shore its thousand echoes cast
Into the night, as if the sea and sky,
And earth, rejoiced with new-born liberty,
For in that name they swore! Bolts were undrawn,
And on the deck, with unaccustomed eye

The captives gazing stood, and every one
Shrank as the inconstant torch upon her countenance shone.

29.
'They were earth's purest children, young and fair,
With eyes the shrines of unawakened thought,
And brows as bright as Spring or Morning, ere
Dark time had there its evil legend wrought
In characters of cloud which wither not.
The change was like a dream to them; but soon
They knew the glory of their altered lot,
In the bright wisdom of youth's breathless noon,
Sweet talk, and smiles, and sighs, all bosoms did attune.

30.
'But one was mute; her cheeks and lips most fair,
Changing their hue like lilies newly blown,
Beneath a bright acacia's shadowy hair,
Waved by the wind amid the sunny noon,
Showed that her soul was quivering; and full soon
That Youth arose, and breathlessly did look
On her and me, as for some speechless boon:
I smiled, and both their hands in mine I took,
And felt a soft delight from what their spirits shook.

CANTO 9.

1.
'That night we anchored in a woody bay,
And sleep no more around us dared to hover
Than, when all doubt and fear has passed away,
It shades the couch of some unresting lover,
Whose heart is now at rest: thus night passed over
In mutual joy: around, a forest grew
Of poplars and dark oaks, whose shade did cover
The waning stars pranked in the waters blue,
And trembled in the wind which from the morning flew.

2.
'The joyous Mariners, and each free Maiden
Now brought from the deep forest many a bough,
With woodland spoil most innocently laden;
Soon wreaths of budding foliage seemed to flow
Over the mast and sails, the stern and prow
Were canopied with blooming boughs, the while

On the slant sun's path o'er the waves we go
Rejoicing, like the dwellers of an isle
Doomed to pursue those waves that cannot cease to smile.

3.
'The many ships spotting the dark blue deep
With snowy sails, fled fast as ours came nigh,
In fear and wonder; and on every steep
Thousands did gaze, they heard the startling cry,
Like Earth's own voice lifted unconquerably
To all her children, the unbounded mirth,
The glorious joy of thy name Liberty!
They heard! As o'er the mountains of the earth
From peak to peak leap on the beams of Morning's birth:

4.
'So from that cry over the boundless hills
Sudden was caught one universal sound,
Like a volcano's voice, whose thunder fills
Remotest skies, such glorious madness found
A path through human hearts with stream which drowned
Its struggling fears and cares, dark Custom's brood;
They knew not whence it came, but felt around
A wide contagion poured they called aloud
On Liberty that name lived on the sunny flood.

5.
'We reached the port. Alas! from many spirits
The wisdom which had waked that cry, was fled,
Like the brief glory which dark Heaven inherits
From the false dawn, which fades ere it is spread,
Upon the night's devouring darkness shed:
Yet soon bright day will burst even like a chasm
Of fire, to burn the shrouds outworn and dead,
Which wrap the world; a wide enthusiasm,
To cleanse the fevered world as with an earthquake's spasm!

6.
'I walked through the great City then, but free
From shame or fear; those toil-worn Mariners
And happy Maidens did encompass me;
And like a subterranean wind that stirs
Some forest among caves, the hopes and fears
From every human soul, a murmur strange
Made as I passed; and many wept, with tears
Of joy and awe, and winged thoughts did range,
And half-extinguished words, which prophesied of change.

7.
'For, with strong speech I tore the veil that hid
Nature, and Truth, and Liberty, and Love,
As one who from some mountain's pyramid
Points to the unrisen sun! the shades approve
His truth, and flee from every stream and grove.
Thus, gentle thoughts did many a bosom fill,
Wisdom, the mail of tried affections wove
For many a heart, and tameless scorn of ill,
Thrice steeped in molten steel the unconquerable will.

8.
'Some said I was a maniac wild and lost;
Some, that I scarce had risen from the grave,
The Prophet's virgin bride, a heavenly ghost:
Some said, I was a fiend from my weird cave,
Who had stolen human shape, and o'er the wave,
The forest, and the mountain, came; some said
I was the child of God, sent down to save
Woman from bonds and death, and on my head
The burden of their sins would frightfully be laid.

9.
'But soon my human words found sympathy
In human hearts: the purest and the best,
As friend with friend, made common cause with me,
And they were few, but resolute; the rest,
Ere yet success the enterprise had blessed,
Leagued with me in their hearts; their meals, their slumber,
Their hourly occupations, were possessed
By hopes which I had armed to overnumber
Those hosts of meaner cares, which life's strong wings encumber.

10.
'But chiefly women, whom my voice did waken
From their cold, careless, willing slavery,
Sought me: one truth their dreary prison has shaken,
They looked around, and lo! they became free!
Their many tyrants sitting desolately
In slave-deserted halls, could none restrain;
For wrath's red fire had withered in the eye,
Whose lightning once was death, nor fear, nor gain
Could tempt one captive now to lock another's chain.

11.
'Those who were sent to bind me, wept, and felt

Their minds outsoar the bonds which clasped them round,
Even as a waxen shape may waste and melt
In the white furnace; and a visioned swound,
A pause of hope and awe the City bound,
Which, like the silence of a tempest's birth,
When in its awful shadow it has wound
The sun, the wind, the ocean, and the earth,
Hung terrible, ere yet the lightnings have leaped forth.

12.
'Like clouds inwoven in the silent sky,
By winds from distant regions meeting there,
In the high name of truth and liberty,
Around the City millions gathered were,
By hopes which sprang from many a hidden lair,
Words which the lore of truth in hues of flame
Arrayed, thine own wild songs which in the air
Like homeless odours floated, and the name
Of thee, and many a tongue which thou hadst dipped in flame.

13.
'The Tyrant knew his power was gone, but Fear,
The nurse of Vengeance, bade him wait the event
That perfidy and custom, gold and prayer,
And whatsoe'er, when force is impotent,
To fraud the sceptre of the world has lent,
Might, as he judged, confirm his failing sway.
Therefore throughout the streets, the Priests he sent
To curse the rebels. To their gods did they
For Earthquake, Plague, and Want, kneel in the public way.

14.
'And grave and hoary men were bribed to tell
From seats where law is made the slave of wrong,
How glorious Athens in her splendour fell,
Because her sons were free, and that among
Mankind, the many to the few belong,
By Heaven, and Nature, and Necessity.
They said, that age was truth, and that the young
Marred with wild hopes the peace of slavery,
With which old times and men had quelled the vain and free.

15.
'And with the falsehood of their poisonous lips
They breathed on the enduring memory
Of sages and of bards a brief eclipse;
There was one teacher, who necessity

Had armed with strength and wrong against mankind,
His slave and his avenger aye to be;
That we were weak and sinful, frail and blind,
And that the will of one was peace, and we
Should seek for nought on earth but toil and misery

16.
'"For thus we might avoid the hell hereafter."
So spake the hypocrites, who cursed and lied;
Alas, their sway was past, and tears and laughter
Clung to their hoary hair, withering the pride
Which in their hollow hearts dared still abide;
And yet obscener slaves with smoother brow,
And sneers on their strait lips, thin, blue and wide,
Said that the rule of men was over now,
And hence, the subject world to woman's will must bow;

17.
'And gold was scattered through the streets, and wine
Flowed at a hundred feasts within the wall.
In vain! the steady towers in Heaven did shine
As they were wont, nor at the priestly call
Left Plague her banquet in the Ethiop's hall,
Nor Famine from the rich man's portal came,
Where at her ease she ever preys on all
Who throng to kneel for food: nor fear nor shame,
Nor faith, nor discord, dimmed hope's newly kindled flame.

18.
'For gold was as a god whose faith began
To fade, so that its worshippers were few,
And Faith itself, which in the heart of man
Gives shape, voice, name, to spectral Terror, knew
Its downfall, as the altars lonelier grew,
Till the Priests stood alone within the fane;
The shafts of falsehood unpolluting flew,
And the cold sneers of calumny were vain,
The union of the free with discord's brand to stain.

19.
'The rest thou knowest. Lo! we two are here
We have survived a ruin wide and deep
Strange thoughts are mine. I cannot grieve or fear,
Sitting with thee upon this lonely steep
I smile, though human love should make me weep.
We have survived a joy that knows no sorrow,
And I do feel a mighty calmness creep

Over my heart, which can no longer borrow
Its hues from chance or change, dark children of to-morrow.

20.
'We know not what will come, yet, Laon, dearest,
Cythna shall be the prophetess of Love,
Her lips shall rob thee of the grace thou wearest,
To hide thy heart, and clothe the shapes which rove
Within the homeless Future's wintry grove;
For I now, sitting thus beside thee, seem
Even with thy breath and blood to live and move,
And violence and wrong are as a dream
Which rolls from steadfast truth, an unreturning stream.

21.
'The blasts of Autumn drive the winged seeds
Over the earth, next come the snows, and rain,
And frosts, and storms, which dreary Winter leads
Out of his Scythian cave, a savage train;
Behold! Spring sweeps over the world again,
Shedding soft dews from her ethereal wings;
Flowers on the mountains, fruits over the plain,
And music on the waves and woods she flings,
And love on all that lives, and calm on lifeless things.

22.
'O Spring, of hope, and love, and youth, and gladness
Wind-winged emblem! brightest, best and fairest!
Whence comest thou, when, with dark Winter's sadness
The tears that fade in sunny smiles thou sharest?
Sister of joy, thou art the child who wearest
Thy mother's dying smile, tender and sweet;
Thy mother Autumn, for whose grave thou bearest
Fresh flowers, and beams like flowers, with gentle feet,
Disturbing not the leaves which are her winding-sheet.

23.
'Virtue, and Hope, and Love, like light and Heaven,
Surround the world. We are their chosen slaves.
Has not the whirlwind of our spirit driven
Truth's deathless germs to thought's remotest caves?
Lo, Winter comes! the grief of many graves,
The frost of death, the tempest of the sword,
The flood of tyranny, whose sanguine waves
Stagnate like ice at Faith the enchanter's word,
And bind all human hearts in its repose abhorred.

24.
'The seeds are sleeping in the soil: meanwhile
The Tyrant peoples dungeons with his prey,
Pale victims on the guarded scaffold smile
Because they cannot speak; and, day by day,
The moon of wasting Science wanes away
Among her stars, and in that darkness vast
The sons of earth to their foul idols pray,
And gray Priests triumph, and like blight or blast
A shade of selfish care o'er human looks is cast.

25.
'This is the winter of the world; and here
We die, even as the winds of Autumn fade,
Expiring in the frore and foggy air.
Behold! Spring comes, though we must pass, who made
The promise of its birth, even as the shade
Which from our death, as from a mountain, flings
The future, a broad sunrise; thus arrayed
As with the plumes of overshadowing wings,
From its dark gulf of chains, Earth like an eagle springs.

26.
'O dearest love! we shall be dead and cold
Before this morn may on the world arise;
Wouldst thou the glory of its dawn behold?
Alas! gaze not on me, but turn thine eyes
On thine own heart it is a paradise
Which everlasting Spring has made its own,
And while drear Winter fills the naked skies,
Sweet streams of sunny thought, and flowers fresh-blown,
Are there, and weave their sounds and odours into one.

27.
'In their own hearts the earnest of the hope
Which made them great, the good will ever find;
And though some envious shade may interlope
Between the effect and it, One comes behind,
Who aye the future to the past will bind
Necessity, whose sightless strength for ever
Evil with evil, good with good must wind
In bands of union, which no power may sever:
They must bring forth their kind, and be divided never!

28.
'The good and mighty of departed ages
Are in their graves, the innocent and free,

Heroes, and Poets, and prevailing Sages,
Who leave the vesture of their majesty
To adorn and clothe this naked world; and we
Are like to them, such perish, but they leave
All hope, or love, or truth, or liberty,
Whose forms their mighty spirits could conceive,
To be a rule and law to ages that survive.

29.
'So be the turf heaped over our remains
Even in our happy youth, and that strange lot,
Whate'er it be, when in these mingling veins
The blood is still, be ours; let sense and thought
Pass from our being, or be numbered not
Among the things that are; let those who come
Behind, for whom our steadfast will has bought
A calm inheritance, a glorious doom,
Insult with careless tread, our undivided tomb.

30.
'Our many thoughts and deeds, our life and love,
Our happiness, and all that we have been,
Immortally must live, and burn and move,
When we shall be no more; the world has seen
A type of peace; and as some most serene
And lovely spot to a poor maniac's eye,
After long years, some sweet and moving scene
Of youthful hope, returning suddenly,
Quells his long madness, thus man shall remember thee.

31.
'And Calumny meanwhile shall feed on us,
As worms devour the dead, and near the throne
And at the altar, most accepted thus
Shall sneers and curses be; what we have done
None shall dare vouch, though it be truly known;
That record shall remain, when they must pass
Who built their pride on its oblivion;
And fame, in human hope which sculptured was,
Survive the perished scrolls of unenduring brass.

32.
'The while we two, beloved, must depart,
And Sense and Reason, those enchanters fair,
Whose wand of power is hope, would bid the heart
That gazed beyond the wormy grave despair:
These eyes, these lips, this blood, seems darkly there

To fade in hideous ruin; no calm sleep
Peopling with golden dreams the stagnant air,
Seems our obscure and rotting eyes to steep
In joy; but senseless death, a ruin dark and deep!

33.
'These are blind fancies, reason cannot know
What sense can neither feel, nor thought conceive;
There is delusion in the world and woe,
And fear, and pain, we know not whence we live,
Or why, or how, or what mute Power may give
Their being to each plant, and star, and beast,
Or even these thoughts. Come near me! I do weave
A chain I cannot break, I am possessed
With thoughts too swift and strong for one lone human breast.

34.
'Yes, yes, thy kiss is sweet, thy lips are warm
O! willingly, beloved, would these eyes,
Might they no more drink being from thy form,
Even as to sleep whence we again arise,
Close their faint orbs in death: I fear nor prize
Aught that can now betide, unshared by thee
Yes, Love when Wisdom fails makes Cythna wise:
Darkness and death, if death be true, must be
Dearer than life and hope, if unenjoyed with thee.

35.
'Alas, our thoughts flow on with stream, whose waters
Return not to their fountain. Earth and Heaven,
The Ocean and the Sun, the Clouds their daughters,
Winter, and Spring, and Morn, and Noon, and Even,
All that we are or know, is darkly driven
Towards one gulf. Lo! what a change is come
Since I first spake but time shall be forgiven,
Though it change all but thee!' She ceased, night's gloom
Meanwhile had fallen on earth from the sky's sunless dome.

36.
Though she had ceased, her countenance uplifted
To Heaven, still spake, with solemn glory bright;
Her dark deep eyes, her lips, whose motions gifted
The air they breathed with love, her locks undight.
'Fair star of life and love,' I cried, 'my soul's delight,
Why lookest thou on the crystalline skies?
O, that my spirit were yon Heaven of night,
Which gazes on thee with its thousand eyes!'

She turned to me and smiled, that smile was Paradise!

CANTO 10.

1.
Was there a human spirit in the steed,
That thus with his proud voice, ere night was gone,
He broke our linked rest? or do indeed
All living things a common nature own,
And thought erect an universal throne,
Where many shapes one tribute ever bear?
And Earth, their mutual mother, does she groan
To see her sons contend? and makes she bare
Her breast, that all in peace its drainless stores may share?

2.
I have heard friendly sounds from many a tongue
Which was not human, the lone nightingale
Has answered me with her most soothing song,
Out of her ivy bower, when I sate pale
With grief, and sighed beneath; from many a dale
The antelopes who flocked for food have spoken
With happy sounds, and motions, that avail
Like man's own speech; and such was now the token
Of waning night, whose calm by that proud neigh was broken.

3.
Each night, that mighty steed bore me abroad,
And I returned with food to our retreat,
And dark intelligence; the blood which flowed
Over the fields, had stained the courser's feet;
Soon the dust drinks that bitter dew, then meet
The vulture, and the wild dog, and the snake,
The wolf, and the hyaena gray, and eat
The dead in horrid truce: their throngs did make
Behind the steed, a chasm like waves in a ship's wake.

4.
For, from the utmost realms of earth came pouring
The banded slaves whom every despot sent
At that throned traitor's summons; like the roaring
Of fire, whose floods the wild deer circumvent
In the scorched pastures of the South; so bent
The armies of the leagued Kings around
Their files of steel and flame; the continent

Trembled, as with a zone of ruin bound,
Beneath their feet, the sea shook with their Navies' sound.

5.
From every nation of the earth they came,
The multitude of moving heartless things,
Whom slaves call men: obediently they came,
Like sheep whom from the fold the shepherd brings
To the stall, red with blood; their many kings
Led them, thus erring, from their native land;
Tartar and Frank, and millions whom the wings
Of Indian breezes lull, and many a band
The Arctic Anarch sent, and Idumea's sand,

6.
Fertile in prodigies and lies; so there
Strange natures made a brotherhood of ill.
The desert savage ceased to grasp in fear
His Asian shield and bow, when, at the will
Of Europe's subtler son, the bolt would kill
Some shepherd sitting on a rock secure;
But smiles of wondering joy his face would fill,
And savage sympathy: those slaves impure,
Each one the other thus from ill to ill did lure.

7.
For traitorously did that foul Tyrant robe
His countenance in lies, even at the hour
When he was snatched from death, then o'er the globe,
With secret signs from many a mountain-tower,
With smoke by day, and fire by night, the power
Of Kings and Priests, those dark conspirators,
He called: they knew his cause their own, and swore
Like wolves and serpents to their mutual wars
Strange truce, with many a rite which Earth and Heaven abhors.

8.
Myriads had come, millions were on their way;
The Tyrant passed, surrounded by the steel
Of hired assassins, through the public way,
Choked with his country's dead: his footsteps reel
On the fresh blood he smiles. 'Ay, now I feel
I am a King in truth!' he said, and took
His royal seat, and bade the torturing wheel
Be brought, and fire, and pincers, and the hook,
And scorpions, that his soul on its revenge might look.

9.
'But first, go slay the rebels, why return
The victor bands?' he said, 'millions yet live,
Of whom the weakest with one word might turn
The scales of victory yet; let none survive
But those within the walls, each fifth shall give
The expiation for his brethren here.
Go forth, and waste and kill!' - 'O king, forgive
My speech,' a soldier answered 'but we fear
The spirits of the night, and morn is drawing near;

10.
'For we were slaying still without remorse,
And now that dreadful chief beneath my hand
Defenceless lay, when on a hell-black horse,
An Angel bright as day, waving a brand
Which flashed among the stars, passed.' - 'Dost thou stand
Parleying with me, thou wretch?' the king replied;
'Slaves, bind him to the wheel; and of this band,
Whoso will drag that woman to his side
That scared him thus, may burn his dearest foe beside;

11.
'And gold and glory shall be his. Go forth!'
They rushed into the plain. Loud was the roar
Of their career: the horsemen shook the earth;
The wheeled artillery's speed the pavement tore;
The infantry, file after file, did pour
Their clouds on the utmost hills. Five days they slew
Among the wasted fields; the sixth saw gore
Stream through the city; on the seventh, the dew
Of slaughter became stiff, and there was peace anew:

12.
Peace in the desert fields and villages,
Between the glutted beasts and mangled dead!
Peace in the silent streets! save when the cries
Of victims to their fiery judgement led,
Made pale their voiceless lips who seemed to dread
Even in their dearest kindred, lest some tongue
Be faithless to the fear yet unbetrayed;
Peace in the Tyrant's palace, where the throng
Waste the triumphal hours in festival and song!

13.
Day after day the burning sun rolled on
Over the death-polluted land it came

Out of the east like fire, and fiercely shone
A lamp of Autumn, ripening with its flame
The few lone ears of corn; the sky became
Stagnate with heat, so that each cloud and blast
Languished and died, the thirsting air did claim
All moisture, and a rotting vapour passed
From the unburied dead, invisible and fast.

14.
First Want, then Plague came on the beasts; their food
Failed, and they drew the breath of its decay.
Millions on millions, whom the scent of blood
Had lured, or who, from regions far away,
Had tracked the hosts in festival array,
From their dark deserts; gaunt and wasting now,
Stalked like fell shades among their perished prey;
In their green eyes a strange disease did glow,
They sank in hideous spasm, or pains severe and slow.

15.
The fish were poisoned in the streams; the birds
In the green woods perished; the insect race
Was withered up; the scattered flocks and herds
Who had survived the wild beasts' hungry chase
Died moaning, each upon the other's face
In helpless agony gazing; round the City
All night, the lean hyaenas their sad case
Like starving infants wailed; a woeful ditty!
And many a mother wept, pierced with unnatural pity.

16.
Amid the aereal minarets on high,
The Ethiopian vultures fluttering fell
From their long line of brethren in the sky,
Startling the concourse of mankind. Too well
These signs the coming mischief did foretell:
Strange panic first, a deep and sickening dread
Within each heart, like ice, did sink and dwell,
A voiceless thought of evil, which did spread
With the quick glance of eyes, like withering lightnings shed.

17.
Day after day, when the year wanes, the frosts
Strip its green crown of leaves, till all is bare;
So on those strange and congregated hosts
Came Famine, a swift shadow, and the air
Groaned with the burden of a new despair;

Famine, than whom Misrule no deadlier daughter
Feeds from her thousand breasts, though sleeping there
With lidless eyes, lie Faith, and Plague, and Slaughter,
A ghastly brood; conceived of Lethe's sullen water.

18.
There was no food, the corn was trampled down,
The flocks and herds had perished; on the shore
The dead and putrid fish were ever thrown;
The deeps were foodless, and the winds no more
Creaked with the weight of birds, but, as before
Those winged things sprang forth, were void of shade;
The vines and orchards, Autumn's golden store,
Were burned; so that the meanest food was weighed
With gold, and Avarice died before the god it made.

19.
There was no corn in the wide market-place
All loathliest things, even human flesh, was sold;
They weighed it in small scales and many a face
Was fixed in eager horror then: his gold
The miser brought; the tender maid, grown bold
Through hunger, bared her scorned charms in vain;
The mother brought her eldest born, controlled
By instinct blind as love, but turned again
And bade her infant suck, and died in silent pain.

20.
Then fell blue Plague upon the race of man.
'O, for the sheathed steel, so late which gave
Oblivion to the dead, when the streets ran
With brothers' blood! O, that the earthquake's grave
Would gape, or Ocean lift its stifling wave!'
Vain cries throughout the streets thousands pursued
Each by his fiery torture howl and rave,
Or sit in frenzy's unimagined mood,
Upon fresh heaps of dead; a ghastly multitude.

21.
It was not hunger now, but thirst. Each well
Was choked with rotting corpses, and became
A cauldron of green mist made visible
At sunrise. Thither still the myriads came,
Seeking to quench the agony of the flame,
Which raged like poison through their bursting veins;
Naked they were from torture, without shame,
Spotted with nameless scars and lurid blains,

Childhood, and youth, and age, writhing in savage pains.

22.
It was not thirst, but madness! Many saw
Their own lean image everywhere, it went
A ghastlier self beside them, till the awe
Of that dread sight to self-destruction sent
Those shrieking victims; some, ere life was spent,
Sought, with a horrid sympathy, to shed
Contagion on the sound; and others rent
Their matted hair, and cried aloud, 'We tread
On fire! the avenging Power his hell on earth has spread!'

23.
Sometimes the living by the dead were hid.
Near the great fountain in the public square,
Where corpses made a crumbling pyramid
Under the sun, was heard one stifled prayer
For life, in the hot silence of the air;
And strange 'twas, amid that hideous heap to see
Some shrouded in their long and golden hair,
As if not dead, but slumbering quietly
Like forms which sculptors carve, then love to agony.

24.
Famine had spared the palace of the king:
He rioted in festival the while,
He and his guards and priests; but Plague did fling
One shadow upon all. Famine can smile
On him who brings it food, and pass, with guile
Of thankful falsehood, like a courtier gray,
The house-dog of the throne; but many a mile
Comes Plague, a winged wolf, who loathes alway
The garbage and the scum that strangers make her prey.

25.
So, near the throne, amid the gorgeous feast,
Sheathed in resplendent arms, or loosely dight
To luxury, ere the mockery yet had ceased
That lingered on his lips, the warrior's might
Was loosened, and a new and ghastlier night
In dreams of frenzy lapped his eyes; he fell
Headlong, or with stiff eyeballs sate upright
Among the guests, or raving mad did tell
Strange truths; a dying seer of dark oppression's hell.

26.

The Princes and the Priests were pale with terror;
That monstrous faith wherewith they ruled mankind,
Fell, like a shaft loosed by the bowman's error,
On their own hearts: they sought and they could find
No refuge 'twas the blind who led the blind!
So, through the desolate streets to the high fane,
The many-tongued and endless armies wind
In sad procession: each among the train
To his own Idol lifts his supplications vain.

27.
'O God!' they cried, 'we know our secret pride
Has scorned thee, and thy worship, and thy name;
Secure in human power we have defied
Thy fearful might; we bend in fear and shame
Before thy presence; with the dust we claim
Kindred; be merciful, O King of Heaven!
Most justly have we suffered for thy fame
Made dim, but be at length our sins forgiven,
Ere to despair and death thy worshippers be driven.

28.
'O King of Glory! thou alone hast power!
Who can resist thy will? who can restrain
Thy wrath, when on the guilty thou dost shower
The shafts of thy revenge, a blistering rain?
Greatest and best, be merciful again!
Have we not stabbed thine enemies, and made
The Earth an altar, and the Heavens a fane,
Where thou wert worshipped with their blood, and laid
Those hearts in dust which would thy searchless works have weighed?

29.
'Well didst thou loosen on this impious City
Thine angels of revenge: recall them now;
Thy worshippers, abased, here kneel for pity,
And bind their souls by an immortal vow:
We swear by thee! and to our oath do thou
Give sanction, from thine hell of fiends and flame,
That we will kill with fire and torments slow,
The last of those who mocked thy holy name,
And scorned the sacred laws thy prophets did proclaim.'

30.
Thus they with trembling limbs and pallid lips
Worshipped their own hearts' image, dim and vast,
Scared by the shade wherewith they would eclipse

The light of other minds; troubled they passed
From the great Temple; fiercely still and fast
The arrows of the plague among them fell,
And they on one another gazed aghast,
And through the hosts contention wild befell,
As each of his own god the wondrous works did tell.

31.
And Oromaze, Joshua, and Mahomet,
Moses, and Buddh, Zerdusht, and Brahm, and Foh,
A tumult of strange names, which never met
Before, as watchwords of a single woe,
Arose; each raging votary 'gan to throw
Aloft his armed hands, and each did howl
'Our God alone is God!' and slaughter now
Would have gone forth, when from beneath a cowl
A voice came forth, which pierced like ice through every soul.

32.
'Twas an Iberian Priest from whom it came,
A zealous man, who led the legioned West,
With words which faith and pride had steeped in flame,
To quell the unbelievers; a dire guest
Even to his friends was he, for in his breast
Did hate and guile lie watchful, intertwined,
Twin serpents in one deep and winding nest;
He loathed all faith beside his own, and pined
To wreak his fear of Heaven in vengeance on mankind.

33.
But more he loathed and hated the clear light
Of wisdom and free thought, and more did fear,
Lest, kindled once, its beams might pierce the night,
Even where his Idol stood; for, far and near
Did many a heart in Europe leap to hear
That faith and tyranny were trampled down;
Many a pale victim, doomed for truth to share
The murderer's cell, or see, with helpless groan,
The priests his children drag for slaves to serve their own.

34.
He dared not kill the infidels with fire
Or steel, in Europe; the slow agonies
Of legal torture mocked his keen desire:
So he made truce with those who did despise
The expiation, and the sacrifice,
That, though detested, Islam's kindred creed

Might crush for him those deadlier enemies;
For fear of God did in his bosom breed
A jealous hate of man, an unreposing need.

35.
'Peace! Peace!' he cried, 'when we are dead, the Day
Of Judgement comes, and all shall surely know
Whose God is God, each fearfully shall pay
The errors of his faith in endless woe!
But there is sent a mortal vengeance now
On earth, because an impious race had spurned
Him whom we all adore, a subtle foe,
By whom for ye this dread reward was earned,
And kingly thrones, which rest on faith, nigh overturned.

36.
'Think ye, because ye weep, and kneel, and pray,
That God will lull the pestilence? It rose
Even from beneath his throne, where, many a day,
His mercy soothed it to a dark repose:
It walks upon the earth to judge his foes;
And what are thou and I, that he should deign
To curb his ghastly minister, or close
The gates of death, ere they receive the twain
Who shook with mortal spells his undefended reign?

37.
'Ay, there is famine in the gulf of hell,
Its giant worms of fire for ever yawn.
Their lurid eyes are on us! those who fell
By the swift shafts of pestilence ere dawn,
Are in their jaws! they hunger for the spawn
Of Satan, their own brethren, who were sent
To make our souls their spoil. See! see! they fawn
Like dogs, and they will sleep with luxury spent,
When those detested hearts their iron fangs have rent!

38.
'Our God may then lull Pestilence to sleep:
Pile high the pyre of expiation now,
A forest's spoil of boughs, and on the heap
Pour venomous gums, which sullenly and slow,
When touched by flame, shall burn, and melt, and flow,
A stream of clinging fire, and fix on high
A net of iron, and spread forth below
A couch of snakes, and scorpions, and the fry
Of centipedes and worms, earth's hellish progeny!

39.
'Let Laon and Laone on that pyre,
Linked tight with burning brass, perish! then pray
That, with this sacrifice, the withering ire
Of Heaven may be appeased.' He ceased, and they
A space stood silent, as far, far away
The echoes of his voice among them died;
And he knelt down upon the dust, alway
Muttering the curses of his speechless pride,
Whilst shame, and fear, and awe, the armies did divide.

40.
His voice was like a blast that burst the portal
Of fabled hell; and as he spake, each one
Saw gape beneath the chasms of fire immortal,
And Heaven above seemed cloven, where, on a throne
Girt round with storms and shadows, sate alone
Their King and Judge, fear killed in every breast
All natural pity then, a fear unknown
Before, and with an inward fire possessed,
They raged like homeless beasts whom burning woods invest.

41.
'Twas morn. At noon the public crier went forth,
Proclaiming through the living and the dead,
'The Monarch saith, that his great Empire's worth
Is set on Laon and Laone's head:
He who but one yet living here can lead,
Or who the life from both their hearts can wring,
Shall be the kingdom's heir a glorious meed!
But he who both alive can hither bring,
The Princess shall espouse, and reign an equal King.'

42.
Ere night the pyre was piled, the net of iron
Was spread above, the fearful couch below;
It overtopped the towers that did environ
That spacious square; for Fear is never slow
To build the thrones of Hate, her mate and foe;
So, she scourged forth the maniac multitude
To rear this pyramid, tottering and slow,
Plague-stricken, foodless, like lean herds pursued
By gadflies, they have piled the heath, and gums, and wood.

43.
Night came, a starless and a moonless gloom.

Until the dawn, those hosts of many a nation
Stood round that pile, as near one lover's tomb
Two gentle sisters mourn their desolation;
And in the silence of that expectation,
Was heard on high the reptiles' hiss and crawl
It was so deep, save when the devastation
Of the swift pest, with fearful interval,
Marking its path with shrieks, among the crowd would fall.

44.
Morn came, among those sleepless multitudes,
Madness, and Fear, and Plague, and Famine still
Heaped corpse on corpse, as in autumnal woods
The frosts of many a wind with dead leaves fill
Earth's cold and sullen brooks; in silence, still
The pale survivors stood; ere noon, the fear
Of Hell became a panic, which did kill
Like hunger or disease, with whispers drear,
As 'Hush! hark! Come they yet? Just Heaven! thine hour is near!'

45.
And Priests rushed through their ranks, some counterfeiting
The rage they did inspire, some mad indeed
With their own lies; they said their god was waiting
To see his enemies writhe, and burn, and bleed,
And that, till then, the snakes of Hell had need
Of human souls: three hundred furnaces
Soon blazed through the wide City, where, with speed,
Men brought their infidel kindred to appease
God's wrath, and, while they burned, knelt round on quivering knees.

46.
The noontide sun was darkened with that smoke,
The winds of eve dispersed those ashes gray.
The madness which these rites had lulled, awoke
Again at sunset. Who shall dare to say
The deeds which night and fear brought forth, or weigh
In balance just the good and evil there?
He might man's deep and searchless heart display,
And cast a light on those dim labyrinths, where
Hope, near imagined chasms, is struggling with despair.

47.
'Tis said, a mother dragged three children then,
To those fierce flames which roast the eyes in the head,
And laughed, and died; and that unholy men,
Feasting like fiends upon the infidel dead,

Looked from their meal, and saw an Angel tread
The visible floor of Heaven, and it was she!
And, on that night, one without doubt or dread
Came to the fire, and said, 'Stop, I am he!
Kill me!' They burned them both with hellish mockery.

48.
And, one by one, that night, young maidens came,
Beauteous and calm, like shapes of living stone
Clothed in the light of dreams, and by the flame
Which shrank as overgorged, they laid them down,
And sung a low sweet song, of which alone
One word was heard, and that was Liberty;
And that some kissed their marble feet, with moan
Like love, and died; and then that they did die
With happy smiles, which sunk in white tranquillity.

CANTO 11.

1.
She saw me not, she heard me not, alone
Upon the mountain's dizzy brink she stood;
She spake not, breathed not, moved not there was thrown
Over her look, the shadow of a mood
Which only clothes the heart in solitude,
A thought of voiceless depth; she stood alone,
Above, the Heavens were spread; below, the flood
Was murmuring in its caves; the wind had blown
Her hair apart, through which her eyes and forehead shone.

2.
A cloud was hanging o'er the western mountains;
Before its blue and moveless depth were flying
Gray mists poured forth from the unresting fountains
Of darkness in the North: the day was dying:
Sudden, the sun shone forth, its beams were lying
Like boiling gold on Ocean, strange to see,
And on the shattered vapours, which defying
The power of light in vain, tossed restlessly
In the red Heaven, like wrecks in a tempestuous sea.

3.
It was a stream of living beams, whose bank
On either side by the cloud's cleft was made;
And where its chasms that flood of glory drank,

Its waves gushed forth like fire, and as if swayed
By some mute tempest, rolled on HER; the shade
Of her bright image floated on the river
Of liquid light, which then did end and fade
Her radiant shape upon its verge did shiver;
Aloft, her flowing hair like strings of flame did quiver.

4.
I stood beside her, but she saw me not
She looked upon the sea, and skies, and earth;
Rapture, and love, and admiration wrought
A passion deeper far than tears, or mirth,
Or speech, or gesture, or whate'er has birth
From common joy; which with the speechless feeling
That led her there united, and shot forth
From her far eyes a light of deep revealing,
All but her dearest self from my regard concealing.

5.
Her lips were parted, and the measured breath
Was now heard there; her dark and intricate eyes
Orb within orb, deeper than sleep or death,
Absorbed the glories of the burning skies,
Which, mingling with her heart's deep ecstasies,
Burst from her looks and gestures; and a light
Of liquid tenderness, like love, did rise
From her whole frame, an atmosphere which quite
Arrayed her in its beams, tremulous and soft and bright.

6.
She would have clasped me to her glowing frame;
Those warm and odorous lips might soon have shed
On mine the fragrance and the invisible flame
Which now the cold winds stole; she would have laid
Upon my languid heart her dearest head;
I might have heard her voice, tender and sweet;
Her eyes, mingling with mine, might soon have fed
My soul with their own joy. One moment yet
I gazed, we parted then, never again to meet!

7.
Never but once to meet on Earth again!
She heard me as I fled, her eager tone
Sunk on my heart, and almost wove a chain
Around my will to link it with her own,
So that my stern resolve was almost gone.
'I cannot reach thee! whither dost thou fly?

My steps are faint. Come back, thou dearest one
Return, ah me! return!' The wind passed by
On which those accents died, faint, far, and lingeringly.

8.
Woe! Woe! that moonless midnight! Want and Pest
Were horrible, but one more fell doth rear,
As in a hydra's swarming lair, its crest
Eminent among those victims even the Fear
Of Hell: each girt by the hot atmosphere
Of his blind agony, like a scorpion stung
By his own rage upon his burning bier
Of circling coals of fire; but still there clung
One hope, like a keen sword on starting threads uphung:

9.
Not death, death was no more refuge or rest;
Not life, it was despair to be! not sleep,
For fiends and chasms of fire had dispossessed
All natural dreams: to wake was not to weep,
But to gaze mad and pallid, at the leap
To which the Future, like a snaky scourge,
Or like some tyrant's eye, which aye doth keep
Its withering beam upon his slaves, did urge
Their steps; they heard the roar of Hell's sulphureous surge.

10.
Each of that multitude, alone, and lost
To sense of outward things, one hope yet knew;
As on a foam-girt crag some seaman tossed
Stares at the rising tide, or like the crew
Whilst now the ship is splitting through and through;
Each, if the tramp of a far steed was heard,
Started from sick despair, or if there flew
One murmur on the wind, or if some word
Which none can gather yet, the distant crowd has stirred.

11.
Why became cheeks, wan with the kiss of death,
Paler from hope? they had sustained despair.
Why watched those myriads with suspended breath
Sleepless a second night? they are not here,
The victims, and hour by hour, a vision drear,
Warm corpses fall upon the clay-cold dead;
And even in death their lips are wreathed with fear.
The crowd is mute and moveless, overhead
Silent Arcturus shines, 'Ha! hear'st thou not the tread

12.
'Of rushing feet? laughter? the shout, the scream,
Of triumph not to be contained? See! hark!
They come, they come! give way!' Alas, ye deem
Falsely 'tis but a crowd of maniacs stark
Driven, like a troop of spectres, through the dark,
From the choked well, whence a bright death-fire sprung,
A lurid earth-star, which dropped many a spark
From its blue train, and spreading widely, clung
To their wild hair, like mist the topmost pines among.

13.
And many, from the crowd collected there,
Joined that strange dance in fearful sympathies;
There was the silence of a long despair,
When the last echo of those terrible cries
Came from a distant street, like agonies
Stifled afar. Before the Tyrant's throne
All night his aged Senate sate, their eyes
In stony expectation fixed; when one
Sudden before them stood, a Stranger and alone.

14.
Dark Priests and haughty Warriors gazed on him
With baffled wonder, for a hermit's vest
Concealed his face; but when he spake, his tone,
Ere yet the matter did their thoughts arrest,
Earnest, benignant, calm, as from a breast
Void of all hate or terror made them start;
For as with gentle accents he addressed
His speech to them, on each unwilling heart
Unusual awe did fall, a spirit-quelling dart.

15.
'Ye Princes of the Earth, ye sit aghast
Amid the ruin which yourselves have made,
Yes, Desolation heard your trumpet's blast,
And sprang from sleep! dark Terror has obeyed
Your bidding, O, that I whom ye have made
Your foe, could set my dearest enemy free
From pain and fear! but evil casts a shade,
Which cannot pass so soon, and Hate must be
The nurse and parent still of an ill progeny.

16.
'Ye turn to Heaven for aid in your distress;

Alas, that ye, the mighty and the wise,
Who, if ye dared, might not aspire to less
Than ye conceive of power, should fear the lies
Which thou, and thou, didst frame for mysteries
To blind your slaves: consider your own thought,
An empty and a cruel sacrifice
Ye now prepare, for a vain idol wrought
Out of the fears and hate which vain desires have brought.

17.
'Ye seek for happiness alas, the day!
Ye find it not in luxury nor in gold,
Nor in the fame, nor in the envied sway
For which, O willing slaves to Custom old,
Severe taskmistress! ye your hearts have sold.
Ye seek for peace, and when ye die, to dream
No evil dreams: all mortal things are cold
And senseless then; if aught survive, I deem
It must be love and joy, for they immortal seem.

18.
'Fear not the future, weep not for the past.
Oh, could I win your ears to dare be now
Glorious, and great, and calm! that ye would cast
Into the dust those symbols of your woe,
Purple, and gold, and steel! that ye would go
Proclaiming to the nations whence ye came,
That Want, and Plague, and Fear, from slavery flow;
And that mankind is free, and that the shame
Of royalty and faith is lost in freedom's fame!

19.
'If thus, 'tis well, if not, I come to say
That Laon' while the Stranger spoke, among
The Council sudden tumult and affray
Arose, for many of those warriors young,
Had on his eloquent accents fed and hung
Like bees on mountain-flowers; they knew the truth,
And from their thrones in vindication sprung;
The men of faith and law then without ruth
Drew forth their secret steel, and stabbed each ardent youth.

20.
They stabbed them in the back and sneered - a slave
Who stood behind the throne, those corpses drew
Each to its bloody, dark, and secret grave;
And one more daring raised his steel anew

To pierce the Stranger. 'What hast thou to do
With me, poor wretch?' Calm, solemn and severe,
That voice unstrung his sinews, and he threw
His dagger on the ground, and pale with fear,
Sate silently his voice then did the Stranger rear.

21.
'It doth avail not that I weep for ye
Ye cannot change, since ye are old and gray,
And ye have chosen your lot, your fame must be
A book of blood, whence in a milder day
Men shall learn truth, when ye are wrapped in clay:
Now ye shall triumph. I am Laon's friend,
And him to your revenge will I betray,
So ye concede one easy boon. Attend!
For now I speak of things which ye can apprehend.

22.
'There is a People mighty in its youth,
A land beyond the Oceans of the West,
Where, though with rudest rites, Freedom and Truth
Are worshipped; from a glorious Mother's breast,
Who, since high Athens fell, among the rest
Sate like the Queen of Nations, but in woe,
By inbred monsters outraged and oppressed,
Turns to her chainless child for succour now,
It draws the milk of Power in Wisdom's fullest flow.

23.
'That land is like an Eagle, whose young gaze
Feeds on the noontide beam, whose golden plume
Floats moveless on the storm, and in the blaze
Of sunrise gleams when Earth is wrapped in gloom;
An epitaph of glory for the tomb
Of murdered Europe may thy fame be made,
Great People! as the sands shalt thou become;
Thy growth is swift as morn, when night must fade;
The multitudinous Earth shall sleep beneath thy shade.

24.
'Yes, in the desert there is built a home
For Freedom. Genius is made strong to rear
The monuments of man beneath the dome
Of a new Heaven; myriads assemble there,
Whom the proud lords of man, in rage or fear,
Drive from their wasted homes: the boon I pray
Is this that Cythna shall be convoyed there

Nay, start not at the name America!
And then to you this night Laon will I betray.

25.
'With me do what ye will. I am your foe!'
The light of such a joy as makes the stare
Of hungry snakes like living emeralds glow,
Shone in a hundred human eyes 'Where, where
Is Laon? Haste! fly! drag him swiftly here!
We grant thy boon.' - 'I put no trust in ye,
Swear by the Power ye dread.' - 'We swear, we swear!'
The Stranger threw his vest back suddenly,
And smiled in gentle pride, and said, 'Lo! I am he!'

CANTO 12.

1.
The transport of a fierce and monstrous gladness
Spread through the multitudinous streets, fast flying
Upon the winds of fear; from his dull madness
The starveling waked, and died in joy; the dying,
Among the corpses in stark agony lying,
Just heard the happy tidings, and in hope
Closed their faint eyes; from house to house replying
With loud acclaim, the living shook Heaven's cope,
And filled the startled Earth with echoes: morn did ope

2.
Its pale eyes then; and lo! the long array
Of guards in golden arms, and Priests beside,
Singing their bloody hymns, whose garbs betray
The blackness of the faith it seems to hide;
And see, the Tyrant's gem-wrought chariot glide
Among the gloomy cowls and glittering spears
A Shape of light is sitting by his side,
A child most beautiful. I' the midst appears
Laon, exempt alone from mortal hopes and fears.

3.
His head and feet are bare, his hands are bound
Behind with heavy chains, yet none do wreak
Their scoffs on him, though myriads throng around;
There are no sneers upon his lip which speak
That scorn or hate has made him bold; his cheek
Resolve has not turned pale, his eyes are mild

And calm, and, like the morn about to break,
Smile on mankind, his heart seems reconciled
To all things and itself, like a reposing child.

4.
Tumult was in the soul of all beside,
Ill joy, or doubt, or fear; but those who saw
Their tranquil victim pass, felt wonder glide
Into their brain, and became calm with awe.
See, the slow pageant near the pile doth draw.
A thousand torches in the spacious square,
Borne by the ready slaves of ruthless law,
Await the signal round: the morning fair
Is changed to a dim night by that unnatural glare.

5.
And see! beneath a sun-bright canopy,
Upon a platform level with the pile,
The anxious Tyrant sit, enthroned on high,
Girt by the chieftains of the host; all smile
In expectation, but one child: the while
I, Laon, led by mutes, ascend my bier
Of fire, and look around: each distant isle
Is dark in the bright dawn; towers far and near,
Pierce like reposing flames the tremulous atmosphere.

6.
There was such silence through the host, as when
An earthquake trampling on some populous town,
Has crushed ten thousand with one tread, and men
Expect the second; all were mute but one,
That fairest child, who, bold with love, alone
Stood up before the King, without avail,
Pleading for Laon's life, her stifled groan
Was heard she trembled like one aspen pale
Among the gloomy pines of a Norwegian vale.

7.
What were his thoughts linked in the morning sun,
Among those reptiles, stingless with delay,
Even like a tyrant's wrath? The signal-gun
Roared, hark, again! In that dread pause he lay
As in a quiet dream the slaves obey
A thousand torches drop, and hark, the last
Bursts on that awful silence; far away,
Millions, with hearts that beat both loud and fast,
Watch for the springing flame expectant and aghast.

8.
They fly, the torches fall, a cry of fear
Has startled the triumphant! they recede!
For, ere the cannon's roar has died, they hear
The tramp of hoofs like earthquake, and a steed
Dark and gigantic, with the tempest's speed,
Bursts through their ranks: a woman sits thereon,
Fairer, it seems, than aught that earth can breed,
Calm, radiant, like the phantom of the dawn,
A spirit from the caves of daylight wandering gone.

9.
All thought it was God's Angel come to sweep
The lingering guilty to their fiery grave;
The Tyrant from his throne in dread did leap,
Her innocence his child from fear did save;
Scared by the faith they feigned, each priestly slave
Knelt for his mercy whom they served with blood,
And, like the refluence of a mighty wave
Sucked into the loud sea, the multitude
With crushing panic, fled in terror's altered mood.

10.
They pause, they blush, they gaze, a gathering shout
Bursts like one sound from the ten thousand streams
Of a tempestuous sea: that sudden rout
One checked, who, never in his mildest dreams
Felt awe from grace or loveliness, the seams
Of his rent heart so hard and cold a creed
Had seared with blistering ice but he misdeems
That he is wise, whose wounds do only bleed
Inly for self, thus thought the Iberian Priest indeed,

11.
And others, too, thought he was wise to see,
In pain, and fear, and hate, something divine;
In love and beauty, no divinity.
Now with a bitter smile, whose light did shine
Like a fiend's hope upon his lips and eyne,
He said, and the persuasion of that sneer
Rallied his trembling comrades 'Is it mine
To stand alone, when kings and soldiers fear
A woman? Heaven has sent its other victim here.'

12.
'Were it not impious,' said the King, 'to break

Our holy oath?' - 'Impious to keep it, say!'
Shrieked the exulting Priest: 'Slaves, to the stake
Bind her, and on my head the burden lay
Of her just torments: at the Judgement Day
Will I stand up before the golden throne
Of Heaven, and cry, "To Thee did I betray
An infidel; but for me she would have known
Another moment's joy! the glory be thine own."'

13.
They trembled, but replied not, nor obeyed,
Pausing in breathless silence. Cythna sprung
From her gigantic steed, who, like a shade
Chased by the winds, those vacant streets among
Fled tameless, as the brazen rein she flung
Upon his neck, and kissed his mooned brow.
A piteous sight, that one so fair and young,
The clasp of such a fearful death should woo
With smiles of tender joy as beamed from Cythna now.

14.
The warm tears burst in spite of faith and fear
From many a tremulous eye, but like soft dews
Which feed Spring's earliest buds, hung gathered there,
Frozen by doubt, alas! they could not choose
But weep; for when her faint limbs did refuse
To climb the pyre, upon the mutes she smiled;
And with her eloquent gestures, and the hues
Of her quick lips, even as a weary child
Wins sleep from some fond nurse with its caresses mild,

15.
She won them, though unwilling, her to bind
Near me, among the snakes. When there had fled
One soft reproach that was most thrilling kind,
She smiled on me, and nothing then we said,
But each upon the other's countenance fed
Looks of insatiate love; the mighty veil
Which doth divide the living and the dead
Was almost rent, the world grew dim and pale,
All light in Heaven or Earth beside our love did fail.

16.
Yet, yet, one brief relapse, like the last beam
Of dying flames, the stainless air around
Hung silent and serene, a blood-red gleam
Burst upwards, hurling fiercely from the ground

The globed smoke, I heard the mighty sound
Of its uprise, like a tempestuous ocean;
And through its chasms I saw, as in a swound,
The tyrant's child fall without life or motion
Before his throne, subdued by some unseen emotion.

17.
And is this death? The pyre has disappeared,
The Pestilence, the Tyrant, and the throng;
The flames grow silent, slowly there is heard
The music of a breath-suspending song,
Which, like the kiss of love when life is young,
Steeps the faint eyes in darkness sweet and deep;
With ever-changing notes it floats along,
Till on my passive soul there seemed to creep
A melody, like waves on wrinkled sands that leap.

18.
The warm touch of a soft and tremulous hand
Wakened me then; lo! Cythna sate reclined
Beside me, on the waved and golden sand
Of a clear pool, upon a bank o'ertwined
With strange and star-bright flowers, which to the wind
Breathed divine odour; high above, was spread
The emerald heaven of trees of unknown kind,
Whose moonlike blooms and bright fruit overhead
A shadow, which was light, upon the waters shed.

19.
And round about sloped many a lawny mountain
With incense-bearing forests and vast caves
Of marble radiance, to that mighty fountain;
And where the flood its own bright margin laves,
Their echoes talk with its eternal waves,
Which, from the depths whose jagged caverns breed
Their unreposing strife, it lifts and heaves,
Till through a chasm of hills they roll, and feed
A river deep, which flies with smooth but arrowy speed.

20.
As we sate gazing in a trance of wonder,
A boat approached, borne by the musical air
Along the waves which sung and sparkled under
Its rapid keel, a winged shape sate there,
A child with silver-shining wings, so fair,
That as her bark did through the waters glide,
The shadow of the lingering waves did wear

Light, as from starry beams; from side to side,
While veering to the wind her plumes the bark did guide.

21.
The boat was one curved shell of hollow pearl,
Almost translucent with the light divine
Of her within; the prow and stern did curl
Horned on high, like the young moon supine,
When o'er dim twilight mountains dark with pine,
It floats upon the sunset's sea of beams,
Whose golden waves in many a purple line
Fade fast, till borne on sunlight's ebbing streams,
Dilating, on earth's verge the sunken meteor gleams.

22.
Its keel has struck the sands beside our feet;
Then Cythna turned to me, and from her eyes
Which swam with unshed tears, a look more sweet
Than happy love, a wild and glad surprise,
Glanced as she spake: 'Ay, this is Paradise
And not a dream, and we are all united!
Lo, that is mine own child, who in the guise
Of madness came, like day to one benighted
In lonesome woods: my heart is now too well requited!'

23.
And then she wept aloud, and in her arms
Clasped that bright Shape, less marvellously fair
Than her own human hues and living charms;
Which, as she leaned in passion's silence there,
Breathed warmth on the cold bosom of the air,
Which seemed to blush and tremble with delight;
The glossy darkness of her streaming hair
Fell o'er that snowy child, and wrapped from sight
The fond and long embrace which did their hearts unite.

24.
Then the bright child, the plumed Seraph came,
And fixed its blue and beaming eyes on mine,
And said, 'I was disturbed by tremulous shame
When once we met, yet knew that I was thine
From the same hour in which thy lips divine
Kindled a clinging dream within my brain,
Which ever waked when I might sleep, to twine
Thine image with HER memory dear, again
We meet; exempted now from mortal fear or pain.

25.
'When the consuming flames had wrapped ye round,
The hope which I had cherished went away;
I fell in agony on the senseless ground,
And hid mine eyes in dust, and far astray
My mind was gone, when bright, like dawning day,
The Spectre of the Plague before me flew,
And breathed upon my lips, and seemed to say,
"They wait for thee, beloved!" then I knew
The death-mark on my breast, and became calm anew.

26.
'It was the calm of love for I was dying.
I saw the black and half-extinguished pyre
In its own gray and shrunken ashes lying;
The pitchy smoke of the departed fire
Still hung in many a hollow dome and spire
Above the towers, like night, beneath whose shade
Awed by the ending of their own desire
The armies stood; a vacancy was made
In expectation's depth, and so they stood dismayed.

27.
'The frightful silence of that altered mood,
The tortures of the dying clove alone,
Till one uprose among the multitude,
And said "The flood of time is rolling on;
We stand upon its brink, whilst THEY are gone
To glide in peace down death's mysterious stream.
Have ye done well? They moulder, flesh and bone,
Who might have made this life's envenomed dream
A sweeter draught than ye will ever taste, I deem.

28.
'"These perish as the good and great of yore
Have perished, and their murderers will repent,
Yes, vain and barren tears shall flow before
Yon smoke has faded from the firmament
Even for this cause, that ye who must lament
The death of those that made this world so fair,
Cannot recall them now; but there is lent
To man the wisdom of a high despair,
When such can die, and he live on and linger here.

29.
'"Ay, ye may fear not now the Pestilence,
From fabled hell as by a charm withdrawn;

All power and faith must pass, since calmly hence
In pain and fire have unbelievers gone;
And ye must sadly turn away, and moan
In secret, to his home each one returning;
And to long ages shall this hour be known;
And slowly shall its memory, ever burning,
Fill this dark night of things with an eternal morning.

30.
'"For me that world is grown too void and cold,
Since Hope pursues immortal Destiny
With steps thus slow, therefore shall ye behold
How those who love, yet fear not, dare to die;
Tell to your children this!" Then suddenly
He sheathed a dagger in his heart and fell;
My brain grew dark in death, and yet to me
There came a murmur from the crowd, to tell
Of deep and mighty change which suddenly befell.

31.
'Then suddenly I stood, a winged Thought,
Before the immortal Senate, and the seat
Of that star-shining spirit, whence is wrought
The strength of its dominion, good and great,
The better Genius of this world's estate.
His realm around one mighty Fane is spread,
Elysian islands bright and fortunate,
Calm dwellings of the free and happy dead,
Where I am sent to lead!' These winged words she said,

32.
And with the silence of her eloquent smile,
Bade us embark in her divine canoe;
Then at the helm we took our seat, the while
Above her head those plumes of dazzling hue
Into the winds' invisible stream she threw,
Sitting beside the prow: like gossamer
On the swift breath of morn, the vessel flew
O'er the bright whirlpools of that fountain fair,
Whose shores receded fast, while we seemed lingering there;

33.
Till down that mighty stream, dark, calm, and fleet,
Between a chasm of cedarn mountains riven,
Chased by the thronging winds whose viewless feet
As swift as twinkling beams, had, under Heaven,
From woods and waves wild sounds and odours driven,

The boat fled visibly, three nights and days,
Borne like a cloud through morn, and noon, and even,
We sailed along the winding watery ways
Of the vast stream, a long and labyrinthine maze.

34.
A scene of joy and wonder to behold
That river's shapes and shadows changing ever,
Where the broad sunrise filled with deepening gold
Its whirlpools, where all hues did spread and quiver;
And where melodious falls did burst and shiver
Among rocks clad with flowers, the foam and spray
Sparkled like stars upon the sunny river,
Or when the moonlight poured a holier day,
One vast and glittering lake around green islands lay.

35.
Morn, noon, and even, that boat of pearl outran
The streams which bore it, like the arrowy cloud
Of tempest, or the speedier thought of man,
Which flieth forth and cannot make abode;
Sometimes through forests, deep like night, we glode,
Between the walls of mighty mountains crowned
With Cyclopean piles, whose turrets proud,
The homes of the departed, dimly frowned
O'er the bright waves which girt their dark foundations round.

36.
Sometimes between the wide and flowering meadows,
Mile after mile we sailed, and 'twas delight
To see far off the sunbeams chase the shadows
Over the grass; sometimes beneath the night
Of wide and vaulted caves, whose roofs were bright
With starry gems, we fled, whilst from their deep
And dark-green chasms, shades beautiful and white,
Amid sweet sounds across our path would sweep,
Like swift and lovely dreams that walk the waves of sleep.

37.
And ever as we sailed, our minds were full
Of love and wisdom, which would overflow
In converse wild, and sweet, and wonderful,
And in quick smiles whose light would come and go
Like music o'er wide waves, and in the flow
Of sudden tears, and in the mute caress
For a deep shade was cleft, and we did know,
That virtue, though obscured on Earth, not less

Survives all mortal change in lasting loveliness.

38.
Three days and nights we sailed, as thought and feeling
Number delightful hours, for through the sky
The sphered lamps of day and night, revealing
New changes and new glories, rolled on high,
Sun, Moon and moonlike lamps, the progeny
Of a diviner Heaven, serene and fair:
On the fourth day, wild as a windwrought sea
The stream became, and fast and faster bare
The spirit-winged boat, steadily speeding there.

39.
Steady and swift, where the waves rolled like mountains
Within the vast ravine, whose rifts did pour
Tumultuous floods from their ten thousand fountains,
The thunder of whose earth-uplifting roar
Made the air sweep in whirlwinds from the shore,
Calm as a shade, the boat of that fair child
Securely fled, that rapid stress before,
Amid the topmost spray, and sunbows wild,
Wreathed in the silver mist: in joy and pride we smiled.

40.
The torrent of that wide and raging river
Is passed, and our aereal speed suspended.
We look behind; a golden mist did quiver
When its wild surges with the lake were blended,
Our bark hung there, as on a line suspended
Between two heavens, that windless waveless lake
Which four great cataracts from four vales, attended
By mists, aye feed; from rocks and clouds they break,
And of that azure sea a silent refuge make.

41.
Motionless resting on the lake awhile,
I saw its marge of snow-bright mountains rear
Their peaks aloft, I saw each radiant isle,
And in the midst, afar, even like a sphere
Hung in one hollow sky, did there appear
The Temple of the Spirit; on the sound
Which issued thence, drawn nearer and more near,
Like the swift moon this glorious earth around,
The charmed boat approached, and there its haven found.

NOTE ON THE "REVOLT OF ISLAM", BY MRS. SHELLEY.

Shelley possessed two remarkable qualities of intellect; a brilliant imagination, and a logical exactness of reason. His inclinations led him (he fancied) almost alike to poetry and metaphysical discussions. I say 'he fancied,' because I believe the former to have been paramount, and that it would have gained the mastery even had he struggled against it. However, he said that he deliberated at one time whether he should dedicate himself to poetry or metaphysics; and, resolving on the former, he educated himself for it, discarding in a great measure his philosophical pursuits, and engaging himself in the study of the poets of Greece, Italy, and England. To these may be added a constant perusal of portions of the old Testament, the Psalms, the Book of Job, the Prophet Isaiah, and others, the sublime poetry of which filled him with delight.

As a poet, his intellect and compositions were powerfully influenced by exterior circumstances, and especially by his place of abode. He was very fond of travelling, and ill-health increased this restlessness. The sufferings occasioned by a cold English winter made him pine, especially when our colder spring arrived, for a more genial climate. In 1816 he again visited Switzerland, and rented a house on the banks of the Lake of Geneva; and many a day, in cloud or sunshine, was passed alone in his boat, sailing as the wind listed, or weltering on the calm waters. The majestic aspect of Nature ministered such thoughts as he afterwards enwove in verse. His lines on the Bridge of the Arve, and his "Hymn to Intellectual Beauty", were written at this time. Perhaps during this summer his genius was checked by association with another poet whose nature was utterly dissimilar to his own, yet who, in the poem he wrote at that time, gave tokens that he shared for a period the more abstract and etherealised inspiration of Shelley. The saddest events awaited his return to England; but such was his fear to wound the feelings of others that he never expressed the anguish he felt, and seldom gave vent to the indignation roused by the persecutions he underwent; while the course of deep unexpressed passion, and the sense of injury, engendered the desire to embody themselves in forms defecated of all the weakness and evil which cling to real life.

He chose therefore for his hero a youth nourished in dreams of liberty, some of whose actions are in direct opposition to the opinions of the world; but who is animated throughout by an ardent love of virtue, and a resolution to confer the boons of political and intellectual freedom on his fellow-creatures. He created for this youth a woman such as he delighted to imagine, full of enthusiasm for the same objects; and they both, with will unvanquished, and the deepest sense of the justice of their cause, met adversity and death. There exists in this poem a memorial of a friend of his youth. The character of the old man who liberates Laon from his tower prison, and tends on him in sickness, is founded on that of Doctor Lind, who, when Shelley was at Eton, had often stood by to befriend and support him, and whose name he never mentioned without love and veneration.

During the year 1817 we were established at Marlow in Buckinghamshire. Shelley's choice of abode was fixed chiefly by this town being at no great distance from London, and its neighbourhood to the Thames. The poem was written in his boat, as it floated under the beech groves of Bisham, or during wanderings in the neighbouring country, which is distinguished for peculiar beauty. The chalk hills break into cliffs that overhang the Thames, or form valleys clothed with beech; the wilder portion of the country is rendered beautiful by exuberant vegetation; and the cultivated part is peculiarly fertile. With all this wealth of Nature which, either in the form of gentlemen's parks or soil dedicated to agriculture, flourishes around, Marlow was inhabited (I hope it is altered now) by a very poor population. The women are lacemakers, and lose their health by sedentary labour, for which they were very ill paid. The Poor-laws ground to the dust not only the paupers, but those who had risen just above that state, and were obliged to pay poor-rates. The changes produced by peace following a long war, and a bad harvest, brought with them the most heart-rending evils to the poor. Shelley afforded what alleviation he could. In the winter, while bringing out his poem, he had a severe attack of ophthalmia, caught while visiting the poor cottages. I mention these things, for this minute and active sympathy with his fellow-creatures gives a thousandfold interest to his speculations, and stamps with reality his pleadings for the human race.

The poem, bold in its opinions and uncompromising in their expression, met with many censurers, not only among those who allow of no virtue but such as supports the cause they espouse, but even among those whose opinions were similar to his own. I extract a portion of a letter written in answer to one of these friends. It best details the impulses of Shelley's mind, and his motives: it was written with entire unreserve; and is therefore a precious monument of his own opinion of his powers, of the purity of his designs, and the ardour with which he clung, in adversity and through the valley of the shadow of death, to views from which he believed the permanent happiness of mankind must eventually spring.

'Marlowe, December 11, 1817.

Percy Bysshe Shelley to Mary Godwin.

'I have read and considered all that you say about my general powers, and the particular instance of the poem in which I have attempted to develop them. Nothing can be more satisfactory to me than the interest which your admonitions express. But I think you are mistaken in some points with regard to the peculiar nature of my powers, whatever be their amount. I listened with deference and self-suspicion to your censures of "The Revolt of Islam"; but the productions of mine which you commend hold a very low place in my own esteem; and this reassures me, in some degree at least. The poem was produced by a series of thoughts which filled my mind with unbounded and sustained enthusiasm. I felt the precariousness of my life, and I engaged in this task, resolved to leave some record of myself. Much of what the volume contains was written with the same feeling, as real, though not so prophetic, as the communications of a dying man. I never presumed indeed to consider it anything approaching to faultless; but, when I consider contemporary productions of the same apparent pretensions, I own I was filled with confidence. I felt that it was in many respects a genuine picture of my own mind. I felt that the sentiments were true, not assumed. And in this have I long believed that my power consists; in sympathy, and that part of the imagination which relates to sentiment and contemplation. I am formed, if for anything not in common with the herd of mankind, to apprehend minute and remote distinctions of feeling, whether relative to external nature or the living beings which surround us, and to communicate the conceptions which result from considering either the moral or the material universe as a whole. Of course, I believe these faculties, which perhaps comprehend all that is sublime in man, to exist very imperfectly in my own mind. But, when you advert to my Chancery-paper, a cold, forced, unimpassioned, insignificant piece of cramped and cautious argument, and to the little scrap about "Mandeville", which expressed my feelings indeed, but cost scarcely two minutes' thought to express, as specimens of my powers more favourable than that which grew as it were from "the agony and bloody sweat" of intellectual travail; surely I must feel that, in some manner, either I am mistaken in believing that I have any talent at all, or you in the selection of the specimens of it. Yet, after all, I cannot but be conscious, in much of what I write, of an absence of that tranquillity which is the attribute and accompaniment of power. This feeling alone would make your most kind and wise admonitions, on the subject of the economy of intellectual force, valuable to me. And, if I live, or if I see any trust in coming years, doubt not but that I shall do something, whatever it may be, which a serious and earnest estimate of my powers will suggest to me, and which will be in every respect accommodated to their utmost limits.

A Note On The Poem's Composition

Composed in the neighbourhood of Bisham Wood, near Great Marlow, Bucks, 1817 (April-September 23); printed, with title (dated 1818), "Laon and Cythna; or, The Revolution of the Golden City: A Vision of the Nineteenth Century", October, November, 1817, but suppressed, pending revision, by the publishers, C & J. Ollier. (A few copies had got out, but these were recalled, and some recovered.) Published, with a fresh title-page and twenty-seven cancel-leaves, as "The Revolt of Islam", January 10, 1818.

www.ingramcontent.com/pod-product-compliance
Lightning Source LLC
Chambersburg PA
CBHW071705040426
42446CB00011B/1919